Best wishes,
Dean Faulkner Wells

THE
GHOSTS

of
ROWAN OAK

THE
GHOSTS
of
ROWAN OAK

*William Faulkner's Ghost Stories
for Children*

Recounted by
DEAN FAULKNER WELLS

Illustrated by John F. Davis

YOKNAPATAWPHA PRESS
Oxford, Mississippi

Published by Yoknapatawpha Press
P.O. Box 248, Oxford, Mississippi 38655

Copyright © 1980 by Dean Faulkner Wells

ISBN 0-916242-07-2   L.C. #80-52628

Third printing, 1991.

Printed in the United States of America
Book design by Barney McKee

For Diane, Paige and Jon, for Gillian,
and for Tad and Will and Bok.

Introduction

by

WILLIE MORRIS

D o you remember the stories your grandfather or uncle or
aunt told you when you were little, the ones you always
wanted to hear again and again? Stories told to you on Hallowe'en or Christmas Eve or in the dull hot summers or on
scary winter nights when your imagination was ready for
them? These stories may have produced a fancy and a wonder
that will take you through adulthood, cherished memories
that will last a lifetime.

The man who told these stories to the children in Oxford,
Mississippi, many years ago, was William Faulkner. You may
guess he was a story teller by profession, for he was one of
the greatest writers ever to have lived. Long before he won
the Nobel Prize for Literature in 1950, he created a whole
mythical world of his own, called Yoknapatawpha County,
and peopled it with characters named Uncle Ike McCaslin and
Major de Spain and Lucas Beauchamp and Flem Snopes and
Quentin Compson and Candace Compson and Gavin Stevens
and Chick Mallison and Temple Drake and Buck Hipps and
Joe Christmas and Dilsey. He understood animals, too, and
wrote about an ancient bear named Ben who roamed the
woods with a crooked foot and an unconquerable spirit, and
a hunting dog named Lion, and some crazy spotted horses
who got loose and terrorized the neighborhood. Adults in
Oxford who knew him well called him "Bill," but to the

children he was always "Pappy." The things he wrote were tragic, and sorrowful, and funny, and sometimes his stories would scare you to death.

Dean Faulkner Wells, who has put down here Mr. Bill's ghost stories as he told them to her and her cousin Jill (Mr. Bill's daughter) and her cousin Vicki and the other children of Oxford, is Mr. Bill's niece. She was named after her father Dean, who was Mr. Bill's youngest and favorite brother. Ten years separated the two brothers, but they were very close and enjoyed one another's company in many moods and moments. Dean Swift Faulkner was killed in an airplane crash when he was only twenty-eight.

His daughter, Dean, describes Rowan Oak, and the "Pappy" of her childhood, with a rare eye, and with the Faulkner care and genius for words, and with the emotion of love. Rowan Oak today is just as she pictured it as it once was— beautiful and serene in the daylight hours, full of dancing shadows and ghostly imaginings at night. Every afternoon I take my big black dog Pete there for his run on the grounds. Once we found ourselves there in a wintry twilight. Suddenly, quick as could be, it became dark and forbidding; the magnolias seemed grotesque monsters, and strange sounds rustled in the darkness. My dog Pete, who usually fears nothing, quickened his steps toward the front gate, and then so did I—an adult man and an adult dog getting out of there fast.

Many people have the impression that Mr. Bill was an aloof presence. He put up a PRIVATE sign in his driveway to discourage curious visitors who came to Oxford to have a glimpse of him. But he loved children, and they felt free to play at Rowan Oak whenever they liked, and to ask him to tell a story. This was their privilege, because he was their friend.

The stories he told them weaved a wonderful magic all their own. He told the same stories over and over, but they never tired of hearing them. They also enjoyed retelling them to each other, when Pappy was not at Rowan Oak. In the 1920s he was also a scoutmaster in the Boy Scouts, and told his tales to the young troops around campfires with little encouragement at all. He helped make the small town of Oxford a fine place to grow up in, from the 1920s through the 1950s. He made such an impression on these children that long after they grew up they never forgot his stories, or the occasions on which he told them. He spoke low and rapidly so that they had to lean closer and be very quiet to catch his words, even though they may have known them by heart. He meant to frighten them out of their wits, and he succeeded. It was fun to be scared, and they relished the sleepless nights which often followed.

In these tales about the lovely and doomed Judith, and the werewolf, and the baying hound, Dean Faulkner Wells has recaptured the sorcery of her uncle's story-telling, and the mood and texture of those vanished moments when he told them. After having recounted them for years to her own children, she has saved them for a new generation of young readers. The story of Judith, briefer in Mr. Bill's telling, has been expanded to round out the characters and situation. "The Hound," the concluding story, has appeared previously in varying forms, and is published here as Dean Wells remembers Mr. Bill's having told it to her and to her contemporaries at Rowan Oak.

In memory there resides a beauty, a tenacity, a splendor which enriches and gives meaning to our lives and to those we love who will follow us. The gift of memory is a haunted blessing. Mr. Bill himself once observed that a writer need not be strong on facts, yet he had better be sure of the truth. Memory carries its own responsibilities, and shapes its own deep heart's truths. In recreating from her memory "Pappy's"

9

tales, which he told with slightly different embellishments over more than a decade, Dean Faulkner Wells has evoked for us children of all ages those universal truths to which her uncle devoted his life.

The University of Mississippi
Oxford, Springtime, 1980

Rowan Oak

Rowan Oak

THE house stands far off Old Taylor Road in Oxford, Mississippi, hidden behind long rows of tall cedar trees. The driveway which leads up to the house is dirt, marred by deep ruts and holes; and on each side grow tangled brambles of honeysuckle and blackberry thickets. The house cannot be seen from the street, but at the end of the driveway, it looms big, and white, and beautiful. It looks as if it has been there forever, its two story wooden frame rising so high that the second story balcony looks into the very tops of the cedar trees.

In daylight, you would love this house. Sunshine streams through the tall windows into the large, airy, high ceilinged rooms which offer plenty of places to play. There is ample space on the front parlor rug for a dozen children to sit cross-legged in a circle and play card games like "Spit" and "Spoons"; there is an open fireplace in the library, large bedrooms upstairs for spend-the-night parties, secluded places to sit and read and think. The grounds surrounding the house are paradise: the croquet wickets stay in place from late spring until school starts in the fall; a ping pong table stands under the portecochere; in the front yard wild grape vines, some of them as thick as a man's arm, trail from the tops of the magnolia trees to the ground, providing natural swings. The tall trees and sand gulleys in the uncleared acres that border the

house lend themselves to endless Saturday outdoor games—
"kick the can" and "capture the flag"—and there are secret
mossy glades for a noon meal of Indian cornbread cooked in a
black iron skillet over a small campfire.

The house is called Rowan Oak. Pappy, the last owner of
the house, gave it this name. He knew the Scottish legend
about the magic of the rowan tree, and he believed in its
powers, which are that a branch of the rowan tree nailed to
the barn door will ward off ghosts and witches and evil spirits. Even though no rowan trees grew on his property, he
named his house after the magic tree.

Most of the time, the name alone is enough to guarantee
peace and security to all those who live at Rowan Oak. But
sometimes, when foxfire dances in the deep woods around
the house, when fog swirls around the trunks of the tall cedar
trees, when the old house groans in the wind and a loose
shutter bangs with a lonely sound, the spell of the rowan tree
is not strong enough. It seems then that in the darkness the
spirits roam the grounds at will, moving about in the lonely
moonlight. And some nights, when the wind is high and
an owl calls from the dead oak tree close to the house, and
hounds bay at the full moon far off in the woods, you can
hear the ghosts of the dead straining at the windows and
doors to get inside.

Everything is fine at Rowan Oak, however, as long as it
is daylight. When the sun is shining, the walk up the long
driveway from the gate to the house is pleasant. The cedars
smell good, the packed dirt underfoot feels good, and the
sunlight makes dappled, yellow patterns through the leaves
onto the grass. But when it starts to get dark, everything
changes.

Pappy knew the French phrase for that time of day, for
twilight, the brief moments in each day when golden sunlight gives way to red and purple and blue, and the shadows

grow long, and darkness is soon at hand, when in the dusk it is difficult to tell the difference between a dog and a wolf. They call it *le temps entre chien et loup*—the time between dog and wolf, the time of day when all that is natural and familiar and safe changes quickly into the unnatural, the strange, the frightening. Twilight never lasts long at Rowan Oak. The large magnolia trees that grow west of the driveway shut out the sun's last rays, and the forbidding shadows lengthen until, all too soon, the driveway is in total darkness.

If you stood at that gate at twilight, when the shadows were already long, when the driveway was swiftly darkening, your heart would beat a little faster, your breath would catch in your throat, and, although you might start out walking toward the house at a normal pace, by the time you had taken a few steps, the urge to run would overwhelm you. And just after you passed the fourth cedar tree, you would bolt, running as hard as you could, feeling the wolf at your back, rushing headlong for the brick walk, the house, and safety. But the closer you got, even when you could see the lights shining out of Pappy's library windows onto the front gallery, and the lights from the dining room and kitchen illuminating the east yard, the more terrified you would become. By then you would be out of breath and so scared that the beating of your heart would seem louder than the rapid thuds of your shoes on the driveway, because, in a spot in front of the house, down the brick walk, across the driveway, under the biggest magnolia, the one whose branches swept the ground and reached the sky, the air was awesomely chilled. Judith was buried there.

You would run as hard as you could past the grave, your eyes straight ahead, not daring to look in that direction; you would veer off sharply to the right, dash up the long, moss-covered brick walk, and thunder across the wooden planks of the gallery. You would yank open the heavy front door, slam it behind you, and stand in the welcoming light of the front hall. As your breathing quieted, you would silently congratulate yourself on your safe arrival. Then you would start to listen.

The house would be quiet. Too quiet. What if Pappy was not at home after all? What if nobody was at home? What if the house was empty? You would stand there, holding your breath, hoping for a sound. Then one might come, the low, mournful creak of an empty old house settling for the night. Your mind would reel in terror. If no one in the family was at home, it could mean that Judith was inside the house . . . with you.

If Judith was inside the house, it would not be the first time. One night the windows and doors at Rowan Oak were opened wide to a balmy spring night, when the sweet, heavy scent of the late-blooming narcissus—so like that of gardenias—hung on the air. The magnolia trees were weighted down with buds, the scent of their fragrant flowers blending with the narcissus so that the warm, dark night was washed in perfumes. On a spring night such as this, when fireflies danced in the grass and a full moon was rising, Judith entered the house.

She came in through the open front door, into the brightly lighted downstairs, and moved silently up the staircase to the upstairs bedroom that had belonged to her. Nobody knew that she was there until they heard the faint sounds of footsteps overhead, moving back and forth across her room.

The ghostly walking went on for several moments as Pappy and his family, seated downstairs at the dining room table, listened to the sounds above. Each of them knew that there could be no one upstairs. They listened as the footsteps moved to the front of the house, to the windows that overlooked the front steps. The footsteps paused there, as if someone were staring out into the front yard, looking down the driveway. Then the soft pacing began again.

When Pappy went upstairs to check, even as his footsteps sounded on the staircase, the other footsteps ceased. He passed no one on the staircase, and when he reached the second story of the house, he searched each bedroom carefully, turning on all the lights as he moved from room to room, looking for anyone who could have made the sounds. No one was there.

She came inside other times, too, late at night, sometimes at three or four o'clock in the morning, when the house was dark, when the last coals in the fireplace in the library no longer burned red. Long after the windows and doors of Rowan Oak had been barred against the night, long after everyone in the family was asleep, she entered the front parlor. Her movements were as silent as shadows until her ghostly hands touched the keys of the grand piano that stood in the corner, just inside the parlor door. The haunting sounds of a Chopin waltz drifted up the stairs, the notes loud enough to wake the family who lay sleeping in their beds. Again, when Pappy went downstairs to investigate, the music ceased abruptly. And when he switched on the lights in the parlor, no one was there. The windows were still tightly shut, and the front door was locked from the inside. Yet everyone in the house had heard her music.

If you were growing up in Oxford, Mississippi, your imagination and fantasies would be filled with Judith; and each time you spent the night at Rowan Oak you would beg Pappy to tell the Judith story, especially on Hallowe'en, because this was the night that the Druids had gathered together in England centuries before, their blue painted faces eerie in the light of bonfires as they danced and howled, beat sticks and drums to keep the spirits of the dead underground. You

17

would come in costume, arriving early to escape the long walk down the driveway after dark. As the sun set, no lights were turned on in the house, so that in the coming darkness, it loomed with an unearthly whiteness. The only lights came from candles placed inside two large jack-o-lanterns sitting on either side of the front steps.

On this night of the supernatural, Pappy would sit on the steps with you and the other costumed children clustered around him, all eyes wide in the flickering candlelight. He seemed to belong outdoors. His skin was weathered, tan, and slightly wrinkled; and he smelled of horses and leather, cedars and sunshine, pipe tobacco and bourbon. His eyes were brown, so dark that they seemed black, and the fine lines around them were traced by smiles and sadness. His hair was gray, cropped close to his head, his small mouth nearly hidden beneath his mustache. Even on the steps he sat very straight, his shoulders squared, his legs crossed. His hands were still, except for the occasional, deliberate movements of his pipe, when he tapped it against the steps. His voice was low and soft, and he spoke rapidly, so that you would strain to catch his words, even though you knew the story almost as well as he. You would be drawn to him by the sound of his voice as much as by the magic of his tale.

Judith

Judith

Wᴴᴇɴ Colonel Robert Sheegog, who was a wealthy Irishman, came here to Oxford in 1844, the town was small. South of the courthouse were beautiful acres of wooded land which had been owned by a Chickasaw Indian named E-Ah-Nah-Yea. Sheegog bought this land and hired an English architect, a man named William Turner, to build a house for him.

First, the land had to be cleared. Slaves worked for weeks felling the big oaks and cottonwoods and sycamores, burning out the stumps and clearing away blackberry and honeysuckle thickets. Then the slaves built a clay kiln and began to make bricks of straw and clay for the foundation.

Slowly the structure took shape. The house looked then very much the way it does now—two stories high, in the colonial style, with the parlors on either side of the entrance hall—but the kitchen was located in a separate building behind the house. There were four bedrooms upstairs, just as there are now. These same four wooden columns supported the Grecian roof that shelters the small balcony. The windows upstairs and downstairs were shuttered, and a brick walk led to the front door. There were always the enormous magnolia trees along the driveway in front of the house.

By 1848 the Sheegog family had settled into the house. A daughter was born that year, and Robert Sheegog named her Judith. She was the most important person in his life. He would not leave the house in the mornings until he had watched her nurse feed her breakfast, and he returned to the big house early so that he could spend an hour or so with her, sitting quietly, watching as she played with her toes, cooing softly as if she knew that, because he was with her, nothing could go wrong.

As soon as she was big enough, he took her with him, perched birdlike in front of him on the English saddle, holding onto the reins over his hands. He taught her to love the feel and smell of horses, the names of trees and animals, and he told her stories of Indians and settlers and war. They were inseparable.

Judith was ten years old in 1858, and, though she was a small child, she was as lean and hard as a boy. She had a mane of dark hair caught into braids each morning by her nurse. After a day spent outdoors—with the exception of the few hours passed in fidgety discomfort with her tutor and piano teacher—she would make her way up the long driveway at nightfall, her face and clothes streaked with the stains of grass and dust, strands of hair loosened and curling from the sweat of tree-climbing and races through the woods on foot or mounted on her pony. As she ran up the driveway, more often than not, the hem of her long, full cotton skirt would trail the ground behind her; she would hike it up round her knees and race for the house, well aware that the huge iron dinner bell had long since been sounded and that she was once again late for supper.

In 1861, when Judith was thirteen, the War Between the States began. From this house she walked with her mother and father the mile to the town square early one fall morning to join the other townspeople and watch the handsome, proud young men in Confederate gray ride off to do battle against their countrymen in blue.

When the officer in charge gave the order for the troops to move out, a mighty cheer went up from the crowd, and, over the din, one clear voice was heard. "Damn those Yankees!" It was Judith's. "Damn them, damn them, damn them!" She felt herself being lifted high to her father's shoulder.

"Yes! Damn them, Missy!" he shouted.

But her mother complained, nagging, "Put her down, Robert. Put that girl down now." The mother's voice was high and strained with emotion. "She's not a child anymore. She's much too old to be carried. You look like the old fool that you are!"

Colonel Sheegog did not seem to notice his wife's whispered demands until the last horse disappeared from sight. Then he hugged Judith to him, set her down gently, and turned to face her mother. Judith ignored their sharp exchange of words that continued over her head as she strained to see the last of the troops ride out of sight. The words were so familiar to her now that they held no impact: "spoiled rotten . . . uncontrollable . . . she's my daughter, too . . ." and because the three of them were surrounded in the courtyard by neighbors and friends, they spoke in the same venomous softness that Judith sometimes overheard through her parents' bedroom door long after she was supposed to be asleep.

The war did not touch Judith in its first year, other than to fill her imagination with glorious fancies of brave, gray-coated young men on horseback who rode hell-bent into the face of battle, with no thoughts of their own safety, and certainly without any trace of cowardice, their swords flashing in the sunlight, their mouths opened to give voice to one continuous victory yell. She memorized the exciting, far-away place name of the battle her father described to her: Bull Run, or the Battle of Manassas. There was no worry in his eyes, then, and certainly no fear.

But by the end of 1861, things began to change.

Robert Sheegog was at home, not because he lacked either courage or the desire to serve the Confederacy, but because his eyesight was poor; and the lines in his face deepened as the war news reached Oxford. There was little peace at home then, either. The days were long, beginning before dawn and ending after sunset, and the work was hard inside this big white house and in the fields around it. Most of the men, white and black, were gone away now to places like Kentucky and Virginia and South Carolina, familiar places Judith had read about but which now seemed not only strange and foreign but dangerous. Soap, tallow, cloth, sugar, even salt were scarcities, and they learned to do without them. Though the fine old silver remained on the sideboard in the dining room, it no longer shone. The fingers that had polished it now wielded hoes in the fields, and there was no one in the big house who had the time to notice or the energy to do anything about it.

Always, though, to the people here in Oxford, the war seemed far away. Then in the spring of 1862 it came terrifyingly close. The Union forces were at Shiloh, near Corinth, only ninety miles from here. For three balmy nights in early April of that year—Judith was fourteen then—she sat up late in the front parlor with her mother and father, while the lamp burned low, its wick sputtering and smoking until finally her mother got up and blew it out, and they sat in darkness. A gentle breeze stirred the faintly dusty, worn curtains at the tall windows and brought in the heavy, intoxicating scent of wisteria. They waited for news of the battle.

When word came the next morning, it was grim—news of the battle of Shiloh, and the Bloody Pond, the small, peaceful watering hole for cattle set in the midst of a peach orchard, in full bloom then, which after two days of battle had run red with the blood of the men and boys who had crawled there to quench their thirst (and spilled their lives into its waters), of

24

the repeated charges at The Sunken Road, of the death of General Albert Sidney Johnston. At Shiloh, the South had lost one of the major battles of the war.

Within a matter of days, the train and wagon loads of wounded and dying soldiers began to reach Oxford, both Confederate and Union, the Federal troops held prisoner on the trains. Many died en route and were buried alongside the railroad tracks in shallow, unmarked graves. As the train rolled into the Oxford depot at dawn, the moans of the wounded men sounded above the clangor of the wheels and the hiss of steam.

Judith and her mother and other women of the town came to the station to meet this train. They waited silently, their faces ashen in the dawn, for the train to stop. As the heavy wooden doors slid open, the women gasped at the stench. They moved stiffly toward the boxcars. Judith swallowed hard to quell the sickness she felt rising in her throat. The Confederate soldiers were moved as quickly as possible to the university, where the classrooms had been converted into a hospital. Only a few were left to lie in misery in the cars. They were Union soldiers, and even though wounded, they were kept under guard.

The soldier in charge of the train looked out at the women still standing in the station, their hands and dresses stained dark brown. He asked, "Is Colonel Sheegog about?" He raised his voice to a near hysterical scream. "I've got to have some help here! Where is Sheegog? If not him, then Jacob Thompson. Somebody has got to take charge. I've got to get back!"

Judith's mother spoke. "They're not here, Captain. They've gone up toward Holly Springs. Tell us what to do."

"Take these men home with you. They're helpless, you see. They won't give you any trouble. They're under house arrest until we can get them to Andersonville." He was already moving backward out of the station yard. "Just hold

25

them till somebody comes for them." Before they could answer, he turned away and disappeared around the corner of the depot.

The three men in blue did not blink or cry out when they were moved into a wagon bed. "I'll drive home," Judith said, as she and her mother climbed into the wagon. "We can't take even one of them, Judith," her mother said softly. "Your father will never hear of it."

Judith urged the tired mule into motion. "We'll take just one, Mama," she said. The young one, she thought, the one with the sun-streaked hair.

Private Michael Johnson, of the Southern Illinois Volunteers, woke for the first time, three weeks later. His head did not hurt, and, after cautiously touching the heavy cloth bandage over his forehead, he looked around the sunlit room. The ceiling was high, fourteen feet, he would guess, and it was obviously a girl's room. The delicate though slightly threadbare, flowered coverlet which lay tossed over his legs, the closet door, ajar so that he could see the skirts of dresses, and most of all, the smell told him so.

The next time he woke, there was a tray beside his bed; the soup was hot, and the door had just closed softy. "Hello?" he called. Suddenly he had become disoriented. Where was he? Where was his regiment? What had happened after the last desperate charge by the Rebels?

"Hello," Judith answered, and entered the room. He looked much better now, she thought, not nearly so peaked, not quite so like a Yankee. And his hair was beautiful.

"Where am I?" he said.

"Oxford, Mississippi. You've been here for three weeks. I've been watching you day and night." She stopped abruptly, blushed, and looked at the floor.

"Am I a prisoner?"

"You certainly are. And as soon as Papa gets home, you'll

26

be sent off to Andersonville. That's what the captain on the train said."

He remembered it all now, the hideous ride, the unending trip when he wished for the blessed relief of death.

"How did I get here?"

"We brought you, my mother and I, because nobody knew what else to do with you."

He stared at her face, and when he spoke, he hoped that the eagerness which stirred within him at her words would not be heard in his voice.

"There's no one here except you and your mother?"

"They've all gone," Judith said. "Old Mr. Wilkins comes to check on you every morning. Papa left for Holly Springs the day you got here, and we haven't heard anything since. But he's all right. He's working in the commissary there. Papa always is all right. There ain't a damn Yankee in this land that could hurt my Papa." She glanced sharply into the handsome face and stammered, "I . . . I didn't mean you!"

She is a beautiful child, he thought. "My name, by the way," he smiled as he spoke, "is Michael Johnson, and yours?"

"I'm Judith Sheegog."

"How old are you, Judy?"

"Nobody ever calls me Judy. My name is Judith, you hear?"

"Yes, Ma'am," he replied. "Judith it will always be."

"I'm fourteen. How old are you?"

"I'm an old man, Judith. I was twenty-one on my last birthday, a century ago, in Illinois."

The talk was easy then, about school and hating it and horses and loving them, about crops and families and hunting and springtime. When Judith's mother called from the bottom of the stairs an hour later and Judith picked up the tray and left the room, Michael Johnson knew how he was going to escape, and Judith Sheegog knew the man she was going to marry.

He was up and about the next day. Judith escorted him into the garden over her mother's protestations: "He's a prisoner, Judith. You hear me! And if he decides to leave, we can't stop him. Your father would die if he knew a Yankee was in this house, you know that. If we let him get away—well, I can't even imagine that."

"It's all right, Mama," Judith said. "He doesn't want to get away. Not now."

They walked and talked there in the east garden, and shared secrets and smiles for two days, always in daylight and under the constant vigil of Judith's mother. The gardens were beautiful, though untended that spring, wild flowers growing among the planted varieties, the colors riotous and the smells so heady that sometimes it was hard for Judith to breathe.

On the third day, Michael joined them at the supper table. He was not seated at the head—there was still no other man present—but across from Judith, at Mrs. Sheegog's left. As they finished the last of the cold cornbread and molasses, Michael carefully considered his reply to Mrs. Sheegog's question about his mother: "I can't remember much about her except she seemed so tall, with long, golden hair that she wore up in a bun mostly. Maybe I'm just remembering pictures I've seen of her. Maybe I can't remember her at all."

"How old were you when she died?" Mrs. Sheegog's face shone with concern.

"Two . . . two and a half." Michael hoped his face looked as sad and vulnerable as he meant it to. His mother's memory had never existed for him, much less meant anything to him. Now he sensed that the moment had come for him to make his move.

"It's such a beautiful night," he said. "Could we walk in the garden just a bit? The three of us? We won't have spring in Illinois for at least a month yet." He stopped talking and allowed the silence to fill the dining room. Both women

28

watched him get up from his chair and move slowly, awkwardly, around the table. "But then, of course, the Georgia spring comes early, doesn't it!"

Mrs. Sheegog stared into her plate. Her mind was filled with pictures of the farmhouse somewhere in Illinois, of the son she had never had, of the girl-child she had borne.

"Go now," her voice was soft. "But don't be long. It will be dark soon."

Michael and Judith walked out the east doors of the dining room, into the garden. They heard Mrs. Sheegog moving back and forth between the kitchen and the house, as she cleared away and began to wash the few dishes from their meagre meal. Michael took Judith's hand as they stepped outside the circle of light and shadow cast at irregular intervals as Mrs. Sheegog moved from table to kitchen. They walked through the tall grass, heavy with dew, and the fireflies began to stir in the unseasonably hot night; with the sudden intrusion they swarmed, sparklers swirling around Judith and Michael like a thousand tiny stars.

"Michael, look! They're beautiful! Papa always says . . ."

He pulled her toward him. "Judith? I can't stay here, you know that. I've got to get back where I belong. Just for a while. Then I'll come back. I'll come back for you. Will you help me, please? I can't do this without you."

They stood at the edge of the tall cedars. The fireflies were everywhere. The whole night was on fire.

"What shall I do, Michael?" Judith's voice was a whisper.

"Nothing. Just stand here for a little while. Don't say or do anything. All right? And remember, I'll come back for you." Then he was gone.

Judith stood alone in the darkness. She blinked furiously at the tears that sprang to her eyes. She strained to catch one last glimpse of Michael. She saw nothing except the swirling patterns of fireflies.

Mrs. Sheegog stood equally still in the kitchen, the lamp shaded by her right hand. She, too, stared hard out the window into the night. She thought she heard a soft, muffled sound, a foot carefully placed on the bottom rung of the wood fence that surrounded the barnyard. Then she heard nothing. "He's gone!" She did not realize that she had spoken aloud. "And God speed."

"Mama." Judith spoke from the darkened dining room. Mrs. Sheegog walked the few steps across the yard that separated the kitchen from the main house, the lamp held high. As she entered the dining room, she blew out the lamp. Mother and daughter felt, rather than saw, each other. They did not touch as they moved slowly yet with the sureness born of familiarity through the darkened rooms, up the staircase, into the upstairs hallway. They paused briefly in front of Judith's bedroom and stared, sightless, at the doorway which led to the upstairs balcony, open now for the night breeze. They heard only the soft rustle of the cedars.

"Goodnight, Mama." Judith's voice could barely be heard above the murmur of the wind in the trees.

"Goodnight, Judith."

Again, they did not touch. Each was thankful for the cover of darkness. Neither could have looked into the other's eyes.

Robert Sheegog came home within a week. The furor over the escaped Yankee prisoner, Michael Johnson, was absorbed into the general frenzy of the war news. During the next few months he was all but forgotten in the talk of mounting casualties, lack of supplies, unsuccessful skirmishes, the growing realization and despondency in the South that the war could be lost; and by the end of 1863, Johnson was remembered daily, even hourly, by only two—Judith and her mother. Yet his name was never spoken.

Although the two women—for Judith was a woman by

then, taller than her mother and with a new softness to her body that had not been there a year before—worked side by side the long hours of each day, no confidence was betrayed. Their secret remained unshared, if indeed either knew she held the other's thoughts and hopes and dreams in her heart.

Robert Sheegog became an old man before their very eyes. The defeat of his beloved Southland was a personal loss; he suffered great agonies at the news of each battle. Only his blinding hatred of the Yankees kept him going. As this destructive emotion grew within him, it consumed even the love he had felt for Judith and his land.

In the summer of 1864, terrifying news swept through the town. The Yankees were coming again. Grant had come in the fall of 1862 without damage to town or property, but this time the townspeople could raise little hope that they would escape again the ravages of war. General A. J. "Whiskey" Smith was the commanding general. If the rumors which ran through the small populace were correct, he would arrive on the morrow.

People were at first immobilized by their fear, then driven to frantic haste in the desperate rush to save what they could. Silver was grabbed from sideboards, thrown into croker sacks, and hauled into pastures where women with heavy shovels dug furiously in the hard ground. They must bury it all, and when the silver was hidden, they rushed back to their barns, urged on by the mounting terror, to save the livestock, as precious now as silver to any family that was lucky enough to still own one cow or one pig or one mule. They led them deep into the woods, to hastily built pens, and worked frantically to camouflage these hiding places. By nightfall, though the town was dark and quiet, no one slept.

Judith sat at the long dining room table alone, her hands folded loosely in front of her. She, too, had spent the day at hard labor, but though her back and arms ached, her mind

31

was at peace. She had waited patiently for two very long years. She remembered the days and nights, the hours and minutes when her thoughts had been filled with the memories of the young man with sunshine in his hair, her Yankee, her Michael. He would be here with her tomorrow. He would come. She knew it.

By this time tomorrow, she thought, I will be with him forever. And before she slept, she carefully laid out her one good dress, the white one with the bit of lace she had meticulously saved from her grandmother's handkerchief and sewed at the neckline and sleeves.

The town was overrun by the men in blue before the sun's first rays touched the face of the clock on the courthouse. For the people of Oxford, the day realized all of their fears. At first there had been only rumors, but by mid-afternoon, the people knew that General "Whiskey" Smith was going to burn the town.

Hysteria swept through the square. High-pitched wails of women and children mingled with the coarse shouts of Union soldiers. Blazing torches caught the dry timbers of stores and frame houses, and the clouds of black smoke billowed into the clear blue sky like low-hanging storm clouds. To the near deafening din of screams and cries and shouts were added the crackling and falling of heavy beams. When, for the people of Oxford, the whole universe seemed to have turned red and gold and black and searing, when the whole world seemed on fire, Judith waited.

She had been waiting since long before dawn, dressed, her small carrying case hidden beneath the biggest magnolia, the one down at the end of the front walk, the one she had loved as a child, the one whose branches brush the earth beneath and reach the sky above. But Michael did not come. She had been patient throughout the long morning hours and into the afternoon, as she listened to the sounds of horror, smelled the smoke, and watched the wind deposit soot here on the window sills of the house.

At first she had thought, "He will come, I know it!" And she was serene with the stillness of heart and mind that comes only with believing. But as the day wore on and she sat motionless in the front parlor, staring out the front windows into the driveway, as the shadows of the big trees lengthened, and twilight was at hand, the first nagging, painful, sharp doubt pierced her. "What if he doesn't come?"

She turned her mind from the thought, but not so quickly that it did not cause her throat to ache and her breath to catch. She forced herself to be calm again, and her breathing quieted. The only sound was the grandfather clock in the hall, ticking away the hopes and the dreams of her life. "He will come, he has to," she thought. And then she made the first excuse. "He has not come yet because he cannot get away. He will have to wait until it's dark. He can't come for me, now. He'll be here as soon as he can. He'll be here right after dark."

And then it was dark. Her mother and father came into the house, overcome not only with exhaustion but with despair. They did not see Judith as she sat still as death in the parlor. They did not talk as they made their way up the staircase. Judith's mother did not answer her father when he said, finally, "Well, at least the scoundrels are gone now. Every last one of them. And they won't be back. There's nothing here for them to come back for."

As they undressed for bed, they did not hear the front door open, nor did they hear Judith's light footsteps on the front steps. They could have seen her if they had looked out the side windows, down into the east garden, because she stood there for a very long time, looking around as if she were seeing the summer night for the first time, as if she had never seen the fireflies before, dancing and swirling about her, rising up out of the heavy dew and catching themselves in the cedars. Then she walked to the front yard and knelt beneath the magnolia, just for a moment.

They could have seen her if they had been looking. Or they could have seen the fiery path around her and behind her as she came up the front walk. They might have heard her as she came up the stairs. But they were almost asleep then. So they did not hear her door open and close. They did not hear it open a few minutes later, or hear her footsteps in the hall as she walked to the balcony. They did not hear anything at all, until the sound of the impact of her body crashing and breaking on the front steps jarred them from their beds. They rushed to the balcony and looked down on the body of their daughter.

She lay crumpled and still, like a child's rag doll thrown down in play, the folds of her white dress spread out over the porch, her long dark hair streaming down the steps behind her, her neck broken.

Robert Sheegog dug a shallow grave beneath the magnolia tree that morning, and he buried Judith there. No one from the town came, not even a minister. Nothing was known about the matter until much later. When her body was covered with dirt, Sheegog and his wife walked back up the walk together and entered the house—alone.

When Pappy finished telling the Judith story, you would get ready for what came next. In the breathless hush there on the front gallery of Rowan Oak, the darkness broken only by the low, flickering candles of the two jack-o-lanterns, you would feel the other children in their costumes and masks begin to press closer together.

"Don't anybody want to visit Judith?" Pappy would ask. And you would hold your breath to make sure it would not be you who replied. When someone braver than the rest said,

"I'll go, Pappy," you knew that Pappy would say, "Who'll keep him company?"

The bravest one would take a lighted candle and walk slowly toward the magnolia tree where the narrow, bare grave was. No grass or flowers ever grew on it, not even weeds. Judith had rested beneath the cold earth protected by the magnolia leaves for many years, except, of course, for the times that she came up out of her grave and walked, moved slowly around Rowan Oak, her feet barely touching the dewy grass, her arms outstretched, searching for her lost lover. Hallowe'en was one of those times.

As you and all the other children crowded along the brick walk behind the wavering candle flame, you expected at any moment to see a white figure hovering in the darkness, as always beyond reach of the candlelight. You tried to feel secure in the knowledge that Pappy was sitting and watching on the front steps behind you, but adults could not be trusted any more than children at Rowan Oak at Hallowe'en, not even Pappy. If you turned and looked, he would be gone.

As you came nearer and nearer to the grave, you hoped with all your heart that Judith would not blow out the candle and leave you in utter darkness. Because when that happened, as it always did, there was a dreadful moment when your eyes opened wide to focus in the pitch black night, and you alone saw Judith walking toward you.

Then everybody else saw her, and everybody ran.

The Werewolf

The Werewolf

I N summertime and in the early fall, you would have gone to Rowan Oak with the other children that Pappy gathered for hayrides. When you got there, the wagon bed would be filled with hay, and you would scramble up eagerly, ready for the long ride, the bonfire, the picnic supper, and the stories. You would be perfectly content to be on your way, as the wagon rolled down the soft, sandy, rutted road, the sounds of the mules' hooves pacing off your progress. You would listen as Pappy pointed out the constellations. "Look to your right," he would say, "and just about one index finger above the horizon you'll see Orion." Then he would tell you about Halley's comet and other stories of the stars.

Usually the ride took about forty-five minutes. The wagon would creak along over a long, sloping hill, and as it reached the bottom, Pappy would say, "This looks like a good place!" Andrew would drive the team into a clearing, and everybody would pile out of the wagon. Before you could scatter to explore the dark woods, Pappy would have you gathering small sticks for kindling, while the big boys would drag in heavy branches from fallen trees. Soon, a bonfire blazed in the night, lighting your way to find the long, thin, pointed sticks for roasting wieners.

After the picnic, when the fire burned low and everything became quiet, you would watch the red sparks bursting out of the coals and drifting upward like tiny red stars. The only sounds would be the crackling of the logs, the last, harsh cries of the katydids and the nightbirds. Then, when stomachs were full, when feet and knees were warmed by the fire, it would be time for Pappy to tell a story.

IN a small village in England, the train station was the focal point of the surrounding countryside, the village's lifeline to civilization. The station itself was a tiny, one-room brick building with four windows and a door that faced the tracks. In the center of the room was a black, pot-bellied stove. Trains came through only twice a day, once at noon and again at four o'clock in the morning.

A young man left London one fall afternoon and traveled to this remote village to see an aging aunt who was sick. Although he had not seen her in years, she was his only living relative and he felt an obligation to make the trip. He had boarded the train in Victoria Station early in the evening and had ridden most of the night, slightly bored and restless at the seemingly endless journey.

The farther he traveled away from London, the more desolate the countryside and the intermittent villages became. When he finally reached his destination a few hours before dawn, he was the only passenger to get off the train at this lonely, forbidding stop. He expected someone, a friend of his aunt's perhaps, to fetch him. The village was at least two miles away, he remembered, accessible only by a rough and unclearly marked path. The thought of undertaking this trek alone in the dark, even though the moon was full, was no more tempting than the thought of entering the black and empty station. A vague feeling of uneasiness crept over him, as he paced back and forth on the deserted platform, trying to decide whether to strike out on his own for his aunt's house or to wait there and hope someone came for him. As he stood staring impatiently into the blackness, clouds rolled in, and along with them came the chilling wind and the roiling clouds of fog so dense, so thick, that the full moon which hung over the horizon was quickly obscured.

The young man looked around the deserted station, hoping to find an attendant. No one was in sight. From the high ridge on which the station was built, he looked down into the shrouded valley and wondered at its darkness—why, even so late at night, there should not be a single light gleaming through the fog from a single cottage. Suddenly at his feet a pattern of light fell. A lamp had been lit by unseen hands. Someone was inside the station.

"How nice," he thought. The night had grown colder now, and he shivered inside his greatcoat. A fire would be fine, and company, while he waited, would make the hours until dawn—or until someone came for him—go faster. He turned and walked into the station. A fire was blazing in the stove, which was so hot that the iron door glowed red. A man sat near the stove. His face was dark, his head bowed so that his thick, curly hair shone in the firelight.

"Good evening, good sir!" the young man said, coming to the stove and stretching his hands toward its warmth. "I'm glad to have company on a night like this."

The man said nothing. He sat with his heels drawn up beneath the bench, his long forearms and abnormally large hands draped on his knees. "Perhaps he's deaf," the young man thought.

41

"Good evening!" he said, louder this time. There was still no response. He took a long, appraising glance at the rough, homespun clothes of a woodsman, at the man's rawboned frame; then he moved away, to the far side of the room, and thought that perhaps this fellow might be willing to talk later, or perhaps it wouldn't matter anyway. Somebody would be along soon to take him to his destination.

He settled himself onto a bench under the lamp which hung from a hook on the wall, brought out the newspaper which he already had read twice on the train, and buried himself behind its pages. He found a story that he had missed in his first and second readings and was soon absorbed. A husky, deep voice startled him.

"We've had trouble around these parts. Do you read about it there in your paper?" The woodsman stood up slowly by the stove and stretched himself as though awakening from sleep. The young traveler became aware, with a sudden curiosity, of the man's huge body. His powerful shoulders sloped forward, his arms swung almost to the floor; and, although he had tried momentarily to pull himself erect, his upper torso still leaned forward, bent slightly at the waist. The young man pitied the backwoodsman, who—he imagined—must have grown this way from years of back-breaking labor, or perhaps more likely, as so often happened in remote districts such as this, he had been misshapen at birth, an occasion no doubt unattended by a mid-wife, much less a physician.

"There doesn't seem to be any news in here about this area," the young man answered. His eyes on the newsprint, he was startled by the sudden shadow that fell over the open pages of his newspaper. Somehow, in spite of the woodsman's hulking form and heavy boots, he had crossed the room with a silent quickness that seemed impossible to the young man. He wondered how the bent and gnarled figure—or any human being, for that matter—could move with such stealth and grace. He felt the abnormal warmth of the man's body and looked up into the craggy face with thick eyebrows knitted over deep-set eyes of the palest yellow. The woodsman was breathing through his mouth, in shallow, quick pants.

The young man recoiled, sliding down the bench, putting distance between him and the strange man, who was beginning to make him feel very uncomfortable. He got up and moved quickly to the window. The proximity of the huge man, combined with the heat of the stove, had made him hot, and he began to perspire. The room seemed much smaller than it had, moments before.

Struggling briefly with the rusted catch on the window, the young man forced the window open. The wind had risen. He could hear the trees bending before it with creaks and groans. The clouds scudded across the face of the full moon. He wished that someone would come for him soon.

"It's getting warm in here," he said over his shoulder to the craggy presence at the far end of the room. "Needed some air, hope you don't . . ." As he turned, the cold wind that rushed into the room extinguished the flickering lamp by the door. In the semi-darkness, lit now by the glow from the fire, he felt himself quite alone. He stared hard at the spot where the woodsman had been standing, willed his eyes to become accustomed to the darkness. "Could he have gone?" he thought. "Slipped out the door while my back was turned? What a strange creature he is."

As his eyes searched the darkness, he heard a low, guttural sound that chilled his bones. Something had growled. "Where are you!" he exclaimed, his voice rising in panic. "Are you here?" He stepped backward, bracing his shoulders against the wall. "Speak up, man!"

"Should've been in the paper," the deep, husky voice spoke from the darkness. "Look down into the village."

43

Unwilling to turn his back on this frightening presence, the young man twisted his head to look out the window as he had been told. Moonlight suddenly flooded the station, and the railroad tracks gleamed white; but no lights could be seen in the distant village. It was getting close to dawn, he reasoned, and lamps should have been lit in some of the farmers' cottages. He stared into the dark valley below, where lights should be glowing. The village seemed to have vanished.

"Where is it?" he asked of the woodsman. "It can't have disappeared. There was a village green there, houses, people . . ."

"They're there, all right," came the deep-throated reply from the darkness. "They're there behind barred doors and shuttered windows. At least, the women and their little ones. Their menfolk are climbin' the hills, didn't you hear 'em? They left by the north road, over fifty of 'em, just after you got here."

"What extraordinary hearing!" the young man thought in amazement and growing unease. The other voice continued.

"They been waitin' for this night, they have, for a month or more. They think they'll get him this time."

"Get who?" the young man exclaimed.

"First it was just a few sheep," the woodsman said, as if the young man had not spoken. "Then a few head of cattle." The timbre of the voice began to grow more urgent. "They said it was a wolf. The throats of the beasts was torn, the marks was right. It looked, indeed, like a wolf gone mad, separated from his pack. Then they found the shepherd boy in the hills above his father's cottage. He'd gone out that night to recover a lost sheep, could hear it bleatin' in the distance. He carried his staff and his father's huntin' knife. The moon was full. He had small trouble findin' his way. The sounds of the cryin' lamb led him to a high, open place in the pines. The sheep was down. The black wolf was at its throat. Whilst the boy watched, the cries stopped. The boy stood still, gatherin' his courage. The wolf turned to him. It started circlin' the boy. When he raised his staff, the wolf was upon him. He had not the time to cry out."

The young man's head reeled with unspoken questions. He still could not see the craggy face behind the voice. He had the chilling sense that, in the shadows, the woodsman had begun to pace back and forth, unseen, without making a sound. The voice continued.

"They had thirty days grace from the wolf's attacks. They thought it was gone. Then at the next full moon, it struck again, this time much closer to the village. There have been four since that time—the old couple, man and his woman, on the road after dark; the young woman, fetchin' water from the stream behind her cottage. And the doctor, tendin' the sick. The horse brought him home lyin' in the bottom of the carriage, his throat torn like the rest. But the wolf had not fed on him or any of the others, not even the sheep. Now the men of the village go out every full moon, armed with their guns and axes . . . lookin'."

"You are living in a nightmare!" the young man cried.

"Though they've hit him with their bullets, they failed to bring him down, but they think they'll get him tonight. They've seen his tracks, they say. And some of 'em know. . . ."

"Then why don't they send for outside help?" the young man demanded. "Why don't they organize a constabulary force?"

"Because they know who they're lookin' for." The voice moved closer to the young man. "They know what they be after. They got his print, and they know what kind of wolf he is. The print is always the same, you see. He's missin' a joint on his right front paw. They've made their preparations. Their guns are loaded special. But they may not get him in time."

At his back the young man thought he heard something move outside the window. He turned to shut it, suddenly relieved to be inside, reassured that he was not alone. The woodsman might be strange, but he was certainly of a size to protect them both from what prowled outside in the darkness. He thought he heard a soft rustling of leaves outside the window, as if a large animal was stealing close. In his sudden terror he had wrenched the window in its tracks so that it became jammed.

"Help me!" he cried. He felt his arms weaken from fear. His mind conjured up the image of a huge wolf hurtling its bulk at him through the window, its teeth and claws bared, half-man, half-beast. "Help me!"

A form loomed up over him. Hairy hands grasped the window and forced it down. Breath came hot against his neck. Within the creature's grip, he stared with horror at the hand beside his own. The first joint of the right index finger was missing.

The young man did not even have time to scream.

When Pappy stopped talking, you and the other children around the fire would remain silent and still. You couldn't help feeling the wolf at your back. A log would crackle loudly, and, as if he knew that you could not stand much more, Pappy would suggest that everyone put out the fire, get back into the wagon, and head for home. As always, he would make you clear the campsite so thoroughly that, when the wagon rolled toward home, except for the blackened pieces of firewood, nothing was left lying in the empty field to show that anyone had been there at all.

The Hound

The Hound

On New Year's Eve, the stories would be told again, this time to another generation, to grown-up children who were too old for Hallowe'en parties and hayrides, but who gathered in the library at Rowan Oak and asked Pappy to tell them again. You would be crouched on the dark staircase, in your night clothes, high up and out of sight at first, and then, at the warm sound of voices and the crackle of the fire, you would creep down, one stair at a time, until you were just outside the library door on the bottom step. You could hear every word.

The ritual never varied. They would visit in the library until the witching hour drew close. Then Pappy would offer them a glass of champagne to drink to the new year. Standing beside the fire, he would raise his glass and propose the toast that always began, "Here's to the younger generation . . ."

When he finished, they would drain their glasses and go out onto the gallery to shoot Roman candles and listen to the din of firecrackers exploding and watch the rockets bursting in the night sky above the Square, as Oxford celebrated a new year. Then they would return to the library, settle themselves on chairs or on the floor around the fireplace, and Pappy would begin to tell the stories they knew so well.

THE two men lived far out in the county. The property lines of their farms joined deep in the bottomland which was thick with pines and brambles. They had lived in their nearly identical, weathered one-room shacks, built about a mile apart but out of sight of each other, for over forty years.

The hatred between them had begun so far back in their youth that neither man remembered what had started it. Perhaps it had been a cow, her milk gone bad from bitterweed, or a sow loose in a late garden, destroying the collards or mustard greens; or perhaps it had been a rusted, sagging barbed wire fence, leaning only inches over one side of a property line.

The cause of the hatred was not important, now. It had long since become a part of each man. Both of them lived with it as they would have lived with wives and families, had they had them. They did not see each other often, but each man carried his hatred of his neighbor inside him as he worked to make a crop year after year, plowing or hoeing or weeding, back-breaking labor in a county where the land was red and poor. Together, the two men might have been able to earn a decent living, but alone, the task was impossible.

So each man lived—his shack cold in winter, gaping cracks open to the icy wind, his stomach aching from the hunger that could never be eased by the monotonous diet of fried cornbread and an occasional piece of pork. Each of them was working in his field before sunup and back inside his shack before dark. They slept on cornhusk-filled flour sacks, each man as close to his crumbling stone fireplace as he could safely be, sleeping in his work clothes—overalls bleached white by the sun—removing only his heavy plow shoes before stretching his tired body on the pallet. In work or repose, they looked alike. Their faces were reddened by endless exposure to the sun and wind, their cheeks marred by deep lines. Their bodies were gaunt.

There was only one difference in the two men. One of them had a dog. It was a hound, as thin and lonely as its master.

One summer evening, after a day of hoeing beneath the relentless glare of the white hot sun, of ending each row within speaking distance of each other across the barbed wire fence, of staring and hating with an inner heat which equalled the blasting temperature of the fields, one of the men followed the other to his cabin, unseen. He walked far enough behind so that the sound of his shoes in the dry, crusted furrows did not betray his presence. He waited in a stand of pines until he saw a thin trickle of gray woodsmoke drift out of the chimney. He knew what the man was doing, that he was kneeling in front of the niggardly blaze as his cornbread fried.

The hound lay on the porch, curled against the gray, weathered boards, its head on its paws. As the odor of cornbread drifted out the open door, it licked its chops repeatedly and breathed in short pants; its bony ribcage rose and fell rhythmically.

When the man moved quietly and silently across the bare yard to the front porch, the hound raised its head and growled deep in its throat. The man inside the cabin called, "Hush, dog!" He did not turn away from his skillet over the fire. The other man stole to the doorway and stood beside the hound, which obediently had ceased its growling but did not cease to watch his every movement. The man crept into the shack and looked down on the figure crouched in front of the fire.

From a stack of kindling on the porch, a piece of stove

51

wood came to his hand as naturally as a hoe or shovel. If he thought of anything of all, it was that there was one more bit of work to be done that day before he rested. His hatred for his neighbor, the ingrained pattern of enmity that had become as natural for him as breathing, was no more intense at that moment than it had been that morning, or the day before, or the day before that. He simply walked into the other man's house, and hit him a clean blow on the head with the thick piece of wood.

The other man fell unconscious to the floor, his face pressed against the rough wooden boards. Without pausing, with the same unhurried economy of motion with which he turned at the edge of a row and fitted his plow neatly into the next furrow, the man picked up his neighbor's butcher knife from the hearth and drove it between his ribs into the heart. He felt no triumph, no murderous elation, only the satisfaction of a job well done.

The man sat on his heels, looked into the fire, and began to consider what he was going to do. He hunkered beside the fire long after its ashes were cold. The sun had set and the quarter moon was rising. The room was dark, and the night chill made him shiver. Through the open door he heard the click of the hound's nails as it trotted back and forth relentlessly on the front porch. It periodically uttered an eerie sound, something between a growl and a whimper, but it did not enter the cabin.

It was midnight before the man had made up his mind what he had to do. He struggled to pick up the corpse, which had grown stiff. The dead man now seemed to outweigh him by twenty pounds. He hefted the burden across his shoulders, walked out of the cabin, and descended the worn plank steps. His brogans left a trail of dried clods of dirt. The hound stood at the edge of the porch, watching him intently.

As he headed across the bare packed yard for the pasture

beyond the house, he heard the hound land lightly on the ground, then sensed the beast at his heels. He staggered a few steps, the dead weight making his progress slow and painful. At the woodpile he reached out stealthily with one hand and freed a piece of wood, then waited until the dog stopped beside him, not whining or growling now, just standing steady and quiet, watching. He threw the wood at the hound's head and hit him just above his right shoulder. The dog did not make a sound. The man shouted, "Git! Git on! Git now!"

The hound stared for a long moment, then trotted around the woodpile and disappeared into the brush. The man watched it go, then propped the body by the woodpile and groped in the tall grass for the shovel he expected to find there.

He headed for the place he had thought of while he had hunkered in the cabin. It was a leaf-strewn gully. The soil there was deep and soft and loamy. He dug the grave quickly, with the same methodical rhythm that he hoed his fields every year. He heaved the body into the shallow grave and shoveled the loose earth, the clods breaking open as they struck the body. He stamped the mound flat with his heavy brogans, then spread leaves over the grave. He brushed his hands on the legs of the overalls, picked up the shovel, and started home. In the darkness, he crossed the familiar terrain of the fields until he reached the barbed wire fence which was the property line.

That night he lay on his bed fully clothed as usual, without having bothered even to remove his shoes. Nor had he made a fire. The cabin was cold, and his hunger gnawed at him. He lay very still on the corn-husk mattress, so still that it made no rustling sound beneath him. He was waiting for another sound that he knew would come. He stared up into the darkness and hoped he would not hear it.

Then it began.

Low at first, but gathering volume, the baying of the hound

filled the night. The man listened, and knew where the dog was. It was not at the dead man's cabin. It had followed the scent of death to the grave, where it sat now, its head raised, howling its pain and accusation. The sound carried for miles. The man did not sleep. He knew that the hound would not tire. He had heard it many times, belling the night away hunting coons with its master in the bottom land. Its distinctive and tireless voice would soon alert other neighbors unless it was stopped. He would have to move the body.

It was still dark when he got up and left his cabin. He found the shovel where he had left it, leaning against the side of his shack. His return to the grave was not difficult, for although he could see no better than he could the first time, the sound led him. The dog did not stop howling when the man stood at the top of the gully, nor did its high wail cease when the first handful of dirt clods struck it on the back. It continued to bay until the man rushed down the incline and swung the heavy shovel before him.

The hound bared its fangs and snarled, its hackles raised. The man took a vicious cut with the shovel, caught the dog in the throat, and knocked him to one side with such ferocity that the impact of the blade hitting flesh jarred the man backwards. As he fell, he threw up one arm, expecting to feel the weight of the dog on him at any moment, but the hound lay still.

The man rose and cautiously approached the animal. It lay curled against the bank of the gulley, its forelegs bent beneath its weight. It did not appear to be breathing. When the man knelt over it with the shovel held high above his head, it gave no life signs. The man examined the jagged opening on the dog's neck and the widening stain on its dark coat as the blood poured from the wound.

"If'n it ain't daid now," he muttered to himself, "it's goan be 'fore mawnin'."

Then he took the shovel and began to dig. He forced the blade deep into the already loosened soil and drove it again and again into the earth with the sole of his shoe, not knowing when the metal blade first struck flesh. He stopped when he heard the blade strike bone. He flung the shovel aside and stepped down into the narrow opening. He grabbed the body around the chest and dragged it from the hole. He kicked dirt and leaves back into the hole, refilling it after a fashion, then picked up the body, settled it over his shoulders as he had carried it before, and began to walk toward the dense stand of timber that led into the bottom. He had forgotten the shovel.

In the pine thicket the night was impenetrably black. The trees were big and grew close together. Vines covered the ground between the trunks, and as he staggered along, they seemed to reach out and clutch at his ankles. He fell once, blundering into a blackberry thicket. The sharp thorns tore at his face and hands as he struggled to his feet. The dead man had fallen on top of him, and he had to kick the body away so he could get up. Maneuvering the body amidst the vines in a sort of grotesque dance, he positioned it so that he finally was able to pick it up again and make his way deeper and deeper into the bottomland.

When he felt that he could walk no farther, he let the body slide from his shoulders to the ground and sat down beside it, breathing hard. He waited until he was rested, then leaned forward on his knees and began to dig, using his hands like trowels. The vines fought him, curling around his fingers and wrists. He was forced to wrench them from the ground. Sometimes their roots would not give way, and they would lash through the callouses on his palms like whips. When he reached the leaf mold and smelled its heavy dank odor, he put his head down close to the dirt like a dog and dug in a fury.

The muscles in his shoulders and back were on fire. Because he could see nothing, he had to feel the depth and size

55

of the grave. When he had satisfied himself that it was deep enough to hide the body, he crawled over to the dead man and shoved the corpse along the ground. He hated to touch it again, so he used his feet to roll it into the grave. Again he knelt beside the hole and scooped loose dirt and leaves over the body until it was hidden. He stood on the mound, as before, and pounded down the earth until the ground was flat. Then he scattered leaves and twigs over the bare spot. He was done.

He trudged home under a sky that had begun to lighten. Dawn was breaking as he reached his cabin. He wanted to sleep even more than he wanted to eat, but he knew that he must do neither. It was time for him to be in the fields. He must be there in case anyone came by his farm. He must be seen doing the chores he routinely did, so that nobody would suspect that anything was wrong. He could sleep that night.

Behind his cabin he found his hoe leaning against the back stoop. As he picked it up, he remembered the shovel. "No matter now," he thought. "I'll fetch it home tomorrow. Been needin' a new shovel."

He worked through the day, though his hands were sore and bleeding. He chopped and weeded the small, withered stalks of cotton he had planted in the spring. He knew that this crop would be no better than that of the previous year, but it was all he had. When the sun began to set, he started back to his cabin with the hoe over his shoulder.

He cooked his supper in the heavy black iron skillet that had belonged to his mother. He lit a small fire, mixed a thin watery batter, fried cornbread and boiled coffee. He wished for some fatback or an egg but had neither. When the hoe-cakes and coffee were ready, he hunkered in front of the dying fire. He ate slowly from the skillet, chewing every bite for a long time, staring into the fire. When he had eaten it all, he left the skillet and his tin cup on the hearth and stretched

56

out on his mattress. It was dark now, and his tired body ached for rest. He had just closed his eyes when he heard it.

The sound came from the bottom, from the land of the big trees and vines. It floated up and out of the thick forest, carried across the fields, hung on the night air, filled his cabin. It was the hound. The long, haunting cry traveled for miles.

The man did not move. "It cain't be," he thought desperately. "I done killed that animal. I struck it down with that shovel. I seen the mark." But his heart knew better. The hound was alive.

He lay still. As the hours passed and the howling did not stop, he began to feel terror creep into his bones. With each long, mournful sound his body shivered. There would be a moment of silence when an unbearable hope would rise in him that the hound would not give voice again. Then he would hear it. He knew that others heard it, too. The night passed. Shortly before daybreak the baying miraculously ceased.

When the cabin took on a gray light, he got up. He picked up the hoe where he had left it and went to his field. As the sun rose overhead, the sweat began to stream from his gaunt face. It soaked his thin overalls, ran down his legs and bare ankles into his brogans. Yet he was cold.

He worked in his field all day until once again the sun began to set, and he walked slowly, methodically, back to his cabin. He had not heard the hound all day, which was reason enough for him to hope that it was dead. He prepared his meager supper, ate, and stretched his exhausted body on his corn-husk pallet. He did not take off his shoes.

The moon rose. He was not surprised when the first long howl reached his ears. He had not slept in two days or nights. He would not sleep this night. The fatigue made him unsure whether he was awake or living a nightmare. The sounds grew in volume until he could stand them no longer. Others would be listening as well. There was no time to lose.

He left the cabin and retraced his steps through the dense underbrush, through the pine thickets and thorny brambles. The baying of the hound lent a new quickness to his gait. When he reached the clearing, he saw the dog. It sat bent forward at the edge of the grave, its head lowered, the wound still open. It did not look at the man.

He knelt by the grave and begain to dig with his hands. Within minutes, his broken fingernails scraped against the stiff, unyielding flesh of the dead man's face. He did not try to uncover the body completely. He took hold of the arms and jerked the corpse out of the earth so that the dirt fell away from the legs in huge clods. The hound lifted its head and watched the man struggle to heave the body over his shoulder. Then it followed as he lunged forward, bent under the weight, crashing through the underbrush, careening into trees, careless of his own pain as long as he held onto his burden. He paid no attention to the hound at his heels, nor did he hear distant voices or see flashlights dancing among the trees as men followed his tracks. He plunged headlong into the woods, deeper and deeper, until he could smell the dank pungent odor of the river. He knew what he was looking for.

In the pale moonlight the dead tree loomed ahead of him, tall and white. It had stood on the bank of the river for years, its branches outspread like skeletal arms. A storm had long ago blown away the top of the tree, and its hollow center gaped open to the sky. He shifted the body on his shoulder and began to climb, awkwardly and slowly, resting the corpse on each branch before lugging it to the next. The hound sat on its haunches and watched.

At last he reached the top. He gasped weakly for breath and clutched the body between him and the trunk in a ghastly embrace. The stench from the face so close to his own caused his stomach to heave. He retched and coughed, turned away his face and fought for air. With a final, superhuman effort, he heaved the dead man's body over the top so that the legs dangled inside the tree. Then he let go, expecting the body to slide safely out of sight. To his horror, it dropped only a few feet, so that the head, shoulders, and one arm were still visible above the tree's rim. The pale, dirt-smeared face leered at him in clownish fashion. The man climbed to the top and precariously balanced himself on hands and knees above the body.

He tightly gripped the stiff, upraised hand to steady himself, placed a foot on either shoulder, and bore down with all his weight. He began to bounce on the body, forcing it down inch by inch. The sweat ran into his eyes; his lips chattered with hysterical laughter that sounded like a thin wail. The hound sat silently at the base of the tree. It was then that the man saw the flashlight beams converging on the clearing beside the river.

He shoved downward with a frenzy, and the body disappeared from sight. He climbed out of the hollow tree, nearly falling in his exhaustion, and fumbled with his feet for each branch as he frantically descended with chattering lips. He leapt the last few feet to the ground, fell, scrabbled upright, staggered to the edge of the river, gulping air to restore his calm. He turned his wet, hot face into the glare of the flashlights with a fierce unconcern.

"They cain't catch me now," he thought. "They'll never think to look in that tree. That 'ere dog cain't tell them nothin'."

He was smiling when the sheriff walked up to him and said, "You're under arrest." The sheriff unhooked the heavy steel handcuffs from his belt and held them out. All the flashlight beams shone on the man's face, then swung down to his right arm.

"I might as well as go peaceable," the man thought. "They don't have evidence. They cain't produce a body for evidence. They'll never find it."

59

He held out his left hand to be handcuffed, realizing for the first time that a heavy weight dragged his right arm down. Something was attached to his arm.

The sheriff looked at him with revulsion, jerked his head and said, "Drop it!"

The man slowly raised his right arm to be handcuffed. The heaviness of it amazed and terrified him. He stared with disbelief and horror at what he held in his grasp. In the moving beams of the flashlights, with his arm stretched at full length before him, he saw the stump of the dead man's arm, the dark fingers curled around his own.

The hound bayed once, a single, rising note, and disappeared into the trees.

Afterword

THE last time Pappy and I talked about his ghost stories was my wedding day. It was a clear, golden, Indian summer afternoon of November, and Pappy and I were the last people to leave Rowan Oak. Everyone else had gone to the church. Our driver was waiting for us, and we settled ourselves in the back seat of the car. As the car moved slowly down the driveway, Pappy took my hand. I believe he knew what I was thinking: Rowan Oak had never looked as beautiful, and I felt that I would never be a part of it again.

As we passed Judith's grave I said, "Pappy, was she real?"

He patted my hand and said, "No, Dean, I made her up as a present for Jill and all the other children down here." He was silent until we neared the gate. Then he added, "But I believe in her, don't you?"

If you came to Oxford, Mississippi, now, and stood on Old Taylor Road at the gate to Rowan Oak, you would see the big white house shimmering through the rows of tall cedars.

The difference is that Pappy is dead, the children have grown up and have children of their own, and the house belongs to others. There won't be any more stories told here, no croquet wickets on the lawn in springtime, no campfires in the woods in the fall, no more sounds of children's laughter or tears.

But regardless of the passing of time, if you started to walk up the driveway at twilight, I think you might still hear faint rustlings in the woods, catch a glimpse of shadowy movement, or sense the fleeting presence of vanished faces that keep the past alive, because the very walls of Rowan Oak contain the memories of countless magic evenings, of stories told and re-told, the joy and sorrow of many generations.

I think you might feel all of this if you were here. At least, I wish that you could, because now the ghosts of Rowan Oak belong to you.

Dean Faulkner Wells is the daughter of William Faulkner's youngest brother, Dean Swift Faulkner, a pilot who was killed in a plane crash in 1935. Her stories and articles have appeared in *Parade Magazine, Ladies Home Journal,* and *The Paris Review.* She is the editor of *The Great American Writers' Cookbook.* Recently she edited *The Best of Bad Faulkner* (H.B.J. Books, 1991).

Vintage Northwest Indiana

Yesteryear is Just Around the Corner

By Robert Flood

Country Barn Publishing

120 Laura Lane

Hobart, Indiana 46342

(219) 942-5197

flood70@comcast.net

www.countrybarnpublishing.net

**Dedicated to Lorelei
my loving wife and
loyal "Brickie"**
(Class of '54)

Vintage Northwest Indiana

Yesteryear Is Just Around the Corner

Copyright C 2015 by Robert Flood

ISBN: *9780692572047*

This book may be purchased in quantity at special discounts for educational, fundraising, business or promotional purposes, and customized editions are possible.

For further information call 219-942-5197.

Popular Amish country and the quaint shops
of Shipshewana lie southeast of Elkhart.
(Photo courtesy of Anita Ritenour on Flicker)

Photo courtesy Lake County Parks.

The Contents

Introduction

As Indiana celebrates its bicentennial in 2016, take a moment to let your mind drift back in time and imagine what the property you live on might have been like 200 years ago.

You could have been wandering through miles of deep woodlands, marshes, a clearing here and there, wildlife everywhere. The Potawatomi Indian tribe , not yet relocated to lands west of the Mississippi, still roamed the region their tepees often prominent along the

(Photo courtesy ActiveHistory.com)

riverbanks. French fur trappers had been followed by British occupation, until the years following the American Revolution when the frontier moved west beyond the Appalachians into the Ohio Valley and the northern Midwest.

A half century later this author's ancestors began to migrate to the Far West from states like Illinois, Missouri and Kansas, first by covered wagon, later by transcontinental railroad. The earliest ones arrived in San Bernardino in 1858.

That made this author a native Californian, who grew up in his teenage years on a 52,000-acre cattle and grain ranch located in remote back country directly atop the infamous San Andreas

Fault. I graduated from a one-room school, still operational, one of the last in California. Isolated as we were, one mile down a dead end dirt road, our family slept outdoors under the stars for thirteen straight summers, looking up at the Milky Way and "shooting stars" and soothed to sleep by the creak of an adjacent windmill. In 2014 I self published *Where the Old West Still Hangs Around,* timed for the 125th anniversary of the town of Paso Robles on the central California coast. It has sold more than a thousand copies and was picked up by Costco in San Luis Obispo.

I've lived for decades now in more populated settings, but forgive me if I still tilt to the countryside, looking even in northwest Indiana for those little pockets of wilderness and touches of yesteryear. You'll find some nostalgia in these pages, perhaps reminiscent of late *Post Tribune* newspaper columnist Carrol Vertrees, with whose themes I could often identify, and in a chapter on the rise and fall of the country barn I'll even sidetrack briefly and throw in a story from the Far West.

My wife, on the other hand, is a native Hobart Brickie. She descends in part from those who migrated from the steel mills near Pittsburgh to the mills of northwest Indiana. Her father, Eugene Callaway, worked at the blast furnaces of U.S. Steel for more than forty years. On the cover

of its corporate magazine (above) dated April, 1941, he's flanked by two associates. It was just eight months before the attack on Pearl Harbor.

Though a Hoosier, my wife and I lived in Chicago and its far southern suburbs for more than four decades before moving back to her hometown upon our retirements. Since settling here I've discovered some of the region's historical riches and vintage atmosphere, all "just around the corner."

Hobart's County Line Apple Orchard and rustic style barn, filled with country items of every kind, though not exactly an historical landmark, draws thousands of visitors each year. The more serene old grist mill at Hobart's Deep River Park and its adjacent trading post once patronized by fur trappers and the Potawatomi Indians, takes you back into real history. In the same wooded setting the Deep River Grinders play vintage baseball by the rules of yesteryear.

Roam around and you can still find music on the front porch, your choice of several county fairs, the legacy of John Philip Sousa and the echoes of Hobart's early day legendary band director William Revelli.

One can still canoe or kayak on waters once traveled by fur trappers, examine the buggy that took Abraham Lincoln to the Ford Theatre, re-live the days of the steam locomotive, uncover the history of the Studebaker, climb the stairs of an old lighthouse and visit the site of Indiana's one-time world class ski jump.

I've yet to find a 50,000-acre cattle or grain ranch in Lake , Porter or LaPorte Counties, but there are still many farms out on the countryside, scattered horse properties, some trails to ride, heavy woods along the duneland shores, abundant wetlands and near primitive wilderness to stroll through with recent completion of the Old Savannah trail. And you may be shocked to know a buffalo herd roams on the perimeters of Hobart!

Not all of this may be new to you, but I look for what journalists call "the back stories." This vintage collection is intended for easy reading and designed both for newcomers and old timers. So let these writings take you back into some of northwest Indiana's historical niches of yesteryear.

They're all just around the corner.

Footnote: Post Tribune columnist Jerry Davich suggests nostalgia today is on the wane, perhaps impacted by the internet generation. He could be right, but older generations in particular will be fascinated by the coffee table book, **Memories Along the South Shore,** *just released by The Times Media Company, a pictorial book assembled in part from its newspaper archives.*

Each fall thousands of Sandhill Cranes stop at the Jasper-Pulaski Fish and Wildlife Area below Lake County enroute south for the winter. (Photo: Donald Willin)

The Deep River Grinders at a Sunday afternoon game. A creek in the far outfield and the sugar shack above require special ground rules. (Photo by Micheal Rivers courtesy Lake County Parks.)

Chapter 1:

The Deep River Grinders and Vintage Base Ball by the Creek

By the rules of the 1860s pitchers are 'hurlers', fouls 'tics' and fans are 'cranks.'

It's a beautiful summer day, with only puffy clouds, for old-time base ball. That's right, usage did not compound the word until after 1880. The setting: the idyllic meadow of Hobart's Deep River County Park on the old Sauk Trail, surrounded by woods once the path of Potawatomi Indians and early pioneers. Leaving the parking lot you will probably enter the meadow from a foot bridge over the river.

Blue-shirted players in suspenders jaw with an official wearing a top hat, who happens to be the esteemed umpire. On the field players try to replicate vintage jargon and still debate among themselves the fine points of how the game evolved.

Players use no gloves and wear no protective equipment. More than two hundred fans, oops, we mean "cranks," gather in lawn chairs and at picnic tables along the field's south side. Close by an old time vendor with an ice chest at his feet will sell you a bottle of sarsaparilla. A woman in vintage attire roams the crowd with programs, and you may also see a little boy or girl in period dress.

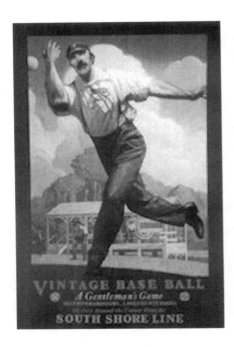

Before each game players are notified they must act like gentlemen at all times, with courteous behavior and respect. Official rules say "there is no cursing, spitting, scratching, consumption of alcohol, chewing of tobacco or wagering. Also, "players shall forbear from commenting on umpire's judgment." Players can even cheer the other team's good plays.

Out in far right field, though, stands an old clapboard sugar shack. Each spring the park collects sap from nearby trees to offer you a taste of Hobart's own maple syrup, emitting the sweet aroma of frontier times gone by. And off beyond, within range of a long ball hitter, lies a meandering river. Or call it a creek. These obstacles demand some special ground rules.

You can play a fly ball off the roof of the sugar shack, but if it rolls under the building's stilts, it's a ground rule double.

Now about that creek. You're supposed to retrieve the ball with a long-handled fish net, but other players will give you help if needed.

I was a quick sideline critic the first time I saw one of the fielders let a fly ball drop in front of him that I thought he could have caught. No, that's often the safest thing to do. You can catch it on the first bounce and it's still an out, though you take the chance that the uneven field will send the ball off another direction.

The umpire does not call balls, but he may call strikes if necessary. He can even ask players or fans to assist in his call. But speak with any disrespect and you'll be fined.

The pitcher delivers the ball underhanded and must try to put it where the batter (oops, "striker,") wants it. The striker is out after three swings or called strikes. Oh, and when you cross the plate, your run is nullified if you forget to ring the bell provided to announce it. Nor are you allowed to slide, lead off, bunt, steal a base or overrun first.

You'll have to back date a lot more of your

current baseball language. It's not a team, but "Club Nine." The shortstop is a "rover," your opponent the "adversary," and runs are "aces." As if these early jocks had their sports lingo all mixed up, the game is a "match."

If it's an out, the term is "player dead." That sounds ominous. The catcher is the "behind." That doesn't sound too good either.

Watch out too for the occasional prank. More than once we've seen a sneaky hurler replace the ball in his hand with a raw egg from his pocket. If it hits the "plate" on a hot day I suppose it could fry, but more often the striker is simply the victim of a yolk. Excuse me.

Oh, and sometimes a fly or line drive can hit food on a picnic bench. If it hit's the ketchup, the team may just be trying to play ketchup ball. Forgive me once more.

These vintage ballplayers do play in a league whose teams scatter from Ohio and Missouri to Illinois, Michigan and Wisconsin. But to a man their "adversaries" all regard Hobart as by far the best setting in which to play, and they say Hobart draws the best crowds. The Grinders are charter members of the Vintage Base Ball Association. Its purpose is to preserve the sport of baseball as it was in its formative years of the mid nineteenth century. Like Civil War re-enactments, they keep history alive.

Let's now add a little more to your vintage base ball glossary. The ball is an apple, pill, horsehide or onion. A sharp grounder is either a bug bruiser or daisy cutter. Outfielders are scouts, infielders base tenders. Pop flies are skyscrapers. Not all the old terminology has died out, like blooper, and midfielder and "leg it" (run!) and

The Deep River Grinders of an earlier year pose for their official team picture. Ask these buffs if they have any old baseball cards to autograph. (Photo courtesy Lake County Parks)

"show a little ginger." An error is a muff but a muffin is an enthusiastic but unskilled player. The outfield is the "garden" and a dew drop is a slow pitch. I'd still like to know why fans are called "cranks." Onlookers behave well enough, so it sounds more like an ill-behaved crowd in the Wrigley Field bleachers.

Each match closes with comments of respect as the teams shake hands down the line, finally raise their caps high to each other and shout in unison three loud "huzzahs" .

The host team (Club Nine), by the way, has to treat the winning team to a meal after the game, but no dining room can quite match the one that the Hobart Grinders offer--Deep River County Park's adjacent visitor center once a community church.

At its side is the old waterwheel of its early day grist mill. So what better name to call themselves than "The Grinders." I bet you thought they specialized in making good coffee.

They're always ready to put their next adversaries "through the mill," as gentlemen, of course, and to grind out another game, oops, match. My final apology.

Sousa in New York (Library of Congress photo)

Chapter 2:

The Old Opera House
And John Philip Sousa

*America's legendary band maestro
staged four concerts in Valparaiso.*

He was "The King of March," an American icon, composer, director of the U.S. Marine Band, "The President's Own" band, under five presidents from Rutherford B. Hayes to Benjamin Harrison. He wrote more than 130 marches, among them America's National March, *The Stars and Stripes Forever.*

Sousa made four appearances in Valparaiso (1893, 1904, 1907, 1914) at its historic opera house, a building still very much alive, constructed in 1893 to honor the veterans of the Civil War. Its walls have echoed with the sounds of vaudeville, opera, drama, political debate and much more. The Marx Brothers appeared here in 1919. Beaulah Bondi, a Valparaiso native, got her start here in theatre in the production of Little Lord Fauntleroy. She played the mother of Jimmy Stewart's character in "It's a Wonderful Life."

Today this theatre hosts a remarkable array of cultural events throughout the year, including Broadway plays, lunchtime cabarets, events for children and more. Its officials pay tribute to the remarkable range of musical and theatrical talent in northwest Indiana on which they can draw.

The Valparaiso Memorial Opera House emits the feel of the past. In its foyer plaques, pictures and newspaper clippings take you back in time. It's not a big auditorium (capacity 354), but it's cozy. One patron described its feel as that of a small Ford Theatre. There are no bad seats, though visibility toward the stage, in my judgment, might have been helped by a little more slant to the floor.

The opera house is registered as a National Landmark, and today a plaque outside the building pays tribute to the hall's historical connections to John Philip Sousa. Briefly, here are some elements of his biographical profile that you may not know.

He was a world class skeet shooter, one of the best who ever lived. Some even consider him the father of the sport.

His father was Portuguese, his mother Bavarian. He was born in Reading, Pennsylvania.

During childhood he studied voice, violin, piano, flute, cornet, baritone horn, trombone and alto horn. He had perfect pitch. He invented the sousaphone, a large brass instrument similar to the tuba, but which directed the sound upward.

His father, a trombonist in the Marine Band, enlisted Sousa as a teenager in the Marine Band to keep him out of a circus band, though the boy did play percussion for P.T. Barnum for about six months. Sousa learned to conduct in a theatrical (pit) orchestra.

In 1888 Sousa wrote *Semper Fedelis,* the official march of the United States Marine Band. Upon later leaving the Marine Band he formed his own Sousa Band, which played for nearly 40 years and staged more than 15,000 concerts.

Mrs. John Philip Sousa. Her fashion era of big hats also required big hatpins, which could be dangerous to another if a woman tilted her head the wrong way. They were once almost outlawed. (Wiki-pedia Commons)

During World War I he led the Marine Band at the Great Lakes Naval Station near Chicago. There he wrote *U.S. Field Artillery,* the official march of the U.S. Army. The most well-known of his other marches written before the turn of the century: *The Gladiator March, The Washington Post, The Thunderer, High School Cadets, The Liberty Bell, Manhattan Beach, King Cotton and El Capitan.*

Sousa also wrote three novels--*The Fifth String, Pipetown Sandy* and *The Transit of Venus.*

He did not like recordings, arguing that "talking machines" were going to ruin the sound of music. The quality of recording in his time

JOHN PHILIP SOUSA'S AMERICA

The Patriot's Life in Images and Words

BY JOHN PHILIP SOUSA IV *with Loras John Schissel*

John Philip Sousa IV, great grandson of the famous bandleader and author of the book above, narrated the Sousa memorial concert at Valparaiso University in 2014.

19

may have justified his views. He was perhaps the first to refer to recordings as "canned music," because cylinder records were sold in cans His band, however, did eventually record.

Sousa wrote marches for several universities, including Illinois, Nebraska, Kansas State and Marquette. He also wrote *Pride of the Wolverines* and *Minnesota March.*

In 1952 Hollywood released its movie, *Stars and Stripes Forever,* a loose biographical account of Sousa's life and career. Clifton Webb plays Sousa. Webb was a native Hoosier, by the way, born in Indianapolis, but bluntly he did not like the Midwest and he worked hard to shed his Indiana accent when he went to Hollywood

Sousa wrote *Presidential Polanaise* for indoor receptions at the White Hose and *Semper Fidelis* for the outdoors. To follow events at the Valparaiso Opera House, click on its website.

The original Studebaker wagon shop in Ohio,
1850, as depicted in an 1893 illustration.
Courtesy of the Studebaker National Museum in
South Bend, Indiana.

Chapter 3:

The Wheelbarrow, the Wagon And the Studebaker Legend

The name rumbled west on covered
wagons and then landed in Indiana.

Studebaker. The name is a part of
northwest Indiana's legacy. It was the make of a
one-time popular car, right. But its name also

rumbled west on half the covered wagons that rolled through sand, rock and river to California.

Think of it--all those pioneers who drove a Studebaker! We must have missed the logo on its "grill" in all those historic images from the archives. Its horsepower? Just count the horses.

The company itself was formalized in 1852, well before the Civil War. It made thousands of wagons for battle, although one very religious Studebaker brother hesitated because he didn't believe in war.

Three Studebaker brothers--Peter, Clement and Henry--sailed from Germany on a Dutch ship in 1738 and settled in York City, Pennsylvania. Descendant John Studebaker later moved to Ohio and taught his sons to make wagons. Two of his sons eventually moved to South Bend, but it was another brother, who'd gone West to the California gold fields, who struck it rich. On gold? No, he made wheelbarrows! Levi Strauss had looked around and seen that these gold miners needed good sturdy pants, anchored by rivets. John Studebaker saw that they also needed wheelbarrows. That's how they carried rock and dirt in those days. In a few short years his business had amassed $8,000.

He was in the right place at the right time. It was the gold rush town of Placerville, first named Hangtown, not exactly a name of endearment.   This author has been there.

His blacksmith brothers made him the wagon for his "Westward Ho." At age 19 the adventurous forty-niner headed out with $65 sewn into his belt, three changes of clothes and a

John Studebaker's wheelbarrow business in the California gold rush town of Placerville helped finance the company's early growth. (Photo courtesy El Dorado County)

Bible. Upon his arrival in the Sierra gold town John took the wise advice of a Mr. Hinds he met, who had sized up John's skills. Build wheelbarrows with me, he urged; you can hunt for gold later. Hinds paid him $10 a wagon. Studebaker soon earned the nickname, "Wheelbarrow Johnny."

The young entrepreneur had stashed away $3000 in a local bank when he got wind the bank might be in financial trouble. He kept an eye on the bank until one night he saw bank officials taking gold out the back door in a wheelbarrow. Studebaker confronted them at gunpoint and demanded his $3,000. He got it.

By the time John's earnings from making wheelbarrows had reached $8,000, these profits could inject a wad of money into the family's South Bend wagon shop, short on cash, and allow the Studebaker brothers to grow the company that would someday become one of the nation's top auto manufacturers. The company had already built its first carriage, described with "fancy hand worked iron trim, the kind of courting buggy any boy or girl would be proud to be seen in."

The company had a spur line to the Lake Shore Railroad that allowed it to ship its product by both rail and steamship. A huge fire in 1872 destroyed the plant, so it was rebuilt. The sprawling operation soon became the largest horse drawn plant in the world. In 1902 Studebaker introduced its first electric (battery powered) car, but later it turned primarily to gasoline. It kept on the cutting edge with its product line: its Big Six in 1918, its President in

BIG-SIX
Touring Car . $1950
F. O. B. Detroit

"This is a Studebaker Year"

1928 and its Land Cruiser in 1934, to name just a few. Its many models awe museum visitors.

Studebaker's glory days, though, peaked around 1949, when as young teenagers my cousin and I would compete to see who could first identify the make of the next oncoming car--on a 40-mile run into town from our ranch out in California's Diablos. Most Fords, Buicks and Chevrolets were gimmes, and I could spot the distinctive grill of a Packard a mile away, but lesser brands like the Hudson, the Nash and the LaSalle were more difficult. In 1947 Studebaker had touted what my cousin dubbed "the forward backward" car, which looked about the same from front or rear, triggering jokes on whether it was coming or going. In an old time radio script it even confused Molly McGee out with Fibber for a drive. Molly screamed that a car was coming right at them! Fibber told her to relax, it was only a Studebaker.

Some say a 1954 price war between Ford and General Motors against which Studebaker could not compete may have started the iconic automaker on its downfall, though company historians say the very size of their operation had sown the seeds of its downfall years earlier. The company finally tried an unsuccessful merger with Packard The last Studebaker came off the assembly line in 1966. A few dealerships by that time also carried the Mercedes Benz.

The more than 100-year saga that started with wagons and wheelbarrows might be called "The rise and fall of the Studebaker." It seems many events in history, great and small, follow such a timeline, no less than the Roman Empire!

Much of the original plant in South Bend is now gone, but not all of it, and you can still re-live its fascinating history with a visit to the Studebaker National Museum there. Models on exhibit even include prototypes that never got off the assembly line.

Studebaker was the first auto maker to establish a proving grounds. It later planted 5,000 trees on its property to spell out its name to those in the air. That "logo" is still plainly visible in a low flyover of South Bend! While Studebaker left its major legacy in Indiana, it also left its footprint in the mountains of California. "Wheelbarrow

Johnny" outlived his brothers and remained the company's honorary president until his death in 1917. Five years earlier John had returned to Placerville, where the town warmly welcomed him as a sort of folk hero. For more than 75 years now the town has held its annual "John M. Studebaker International Wheelbarrow" races in his honor. A marker in town marks the site of his former wheelbarrow shop and a statue of him stands nearby—pushing a wheelbarrow.

This scene from an early advertisement tells you the lady is driving a Studebaker on Chicago's Lake Shore Drive (Studebaker Museum).

The Lake County Courthouse. (Photo by David Flood)

Chapter 4:

Legends of Yesteryear from the Historic Crown Point Courthouse.

Gangster John Dillinger escaped jail and here past celebrities tied the knot.

Ronald Reagan and Jane Wyman got their wedding license here. Gold-tongued orator William Jennings Bryan, running for President, addressed a large crowd from its steps in 1896.

When in 1909 Louis Chevrolet, founder of the automobile bearing his name, won the Cobe Cup Race, first long distance auto race in the nation and precursor to the Indianapolis 500, he accepted the trophy on the Crown Point Courthouse steps. In Las Vegas tradition tens of thousands were married here over the years, including actor Rudolph Valentino, cowboy star Tom Mix, fighter Cassius Clay and singer Michael Jackson. Add also football great Red Grange, fighter Mohammed Ali and two of the Mills brothers. Though hardly celebrities, my wife and I got our own marriage license here.

It has been estimated that at least 175,000 couples have been married at the Lake County Court House over the decades, though the once round-the-clock marriage mayhem tailed off in 1940 when Indiana law required a blood test. It took three days for the return of results.

Each year during its Hometown Festival Crown Point's "Marriage Mill" perpetuates the town's tradition of romance as couples stand at the steps of the Lake court house to marry or reinstate their wedding vows.

It should be clarified that Ronald Reagan, who would later become President, and actress Jane Wyman, though taking out their license in Crown Point, married in Glendale, California. As it turned out, the marriage didn't last.

As for Rudolph Valentino, the younger generation may ask, "Who was he?" It was many decades ago, of course, but we'll call him the Italian born sensation of the silent screen who was known by many as "The Latin Lover." His movie, *Four Horsemen of the Apocalypse,* was the first to earn a million dollars at the box office. Women swooned over him. Men were not so impressed. They preferred a more masculine actor like Douglas Fairbanks.

Upon their marriage by a court house judge, Valentino and his bride stepped out into public sight to the cheers of the curious who had gathered. Word of the event quickly flashed across the country, giving Crown Point, Indiana, a special moment of national fame.

One in the wedding party noted, though, that Valentino seemed as nervous as any typical groom. "There was nothing about his appearance during the ceremony," he said, "that bore out his worldwide reputation of being the cool, calm, deliberate and perfect lover of screen fame."

For his wedding license at Crown Point Valentino registered as Rudolph Guglielmi, but records back in Italy show his full name as Rudolph Alfonso Rafaello Pierre Filbert Guglielmi di Valentino D'Antanqualla in Castelianeta Puglia, Kingdom of Italy!

No celebrity wedding at the Crown Point Court House, however, surpassed the drama that unfolded there on March 3, 1934. On that day infamous gangster John Dillinger, the nation's public enemy #1, broke out of what had been labeled a "foolproof" jail with a hand-carved wooden gun blackened with shoe polish, though one report says he might have sneaked in the gun himself. He tricked a guard into unlocking his cell, took seventeen hostages, then lured the other guards to his cell one by one and locked them in. It was not the final indignity. He then stole the car of Sheriff Lillian Holley. It all left Crown Point highly embarrassed. To no one's surprise it destroyed the sheriff's political future. The episode would have made Barney Fife look like a pro.

Dillinger and his henchmen had just already pulled off a yearlong crime spree of bank robberies in several states and had been charged with the murder of an East Chicago, Indiana, police officer who had shot Dillinger through his bullet-proof vest. Dillinger had successfully returned fire. His notoriety exceeded even names like Baby Face Nelson, Pretty Boy Floyd and Bonnie and Clyde, violent criminals all.

The government said "enough" and J. Edgar Hoover rolled out with his FBI, promptly labeling Dillinger Public Enemy #1. It would be

At the Lake County courthouse in Crown Point, John Dillinger is charged with the murder of police officer O'Malley (AP Photo courtesy U.S. National Archives).

another year before Dillinger would finally be gunned down by authorities as he left the Biograph Theatre on Chicago's Clark Street. I n March, 2008, Crown Point saw this infamous breakout repeated when Universal Studios moved in to film a segment of its movie, *Public Enemies,* starring Johnny Depp as Dillinger and Christian Bale as FBI agent Melvin Purvis. Actress Lili Taylor portrayed the disgraced Sheriff Holley. The filming took three days, and Johnny Depp emerged from the set each evening to shake hands with delighted fans. Universal released the film in June, 2009.

While local folk like tourism, most don't want Dillinger turned into a folk hero. Even some details of the murder charge and the escape are still debated among town residents.

On June, 2013, at the Lake County Fairgrounds Crown Point held its latest Public Enemy Fest to raise money for a local charity. The event showed off the car used by Johnny Depp in the movie and included a prohibition-era costume contest and a vintage car contest. Authorities had even arranged to showcase the original wooden gun used by Dillinger in his great escape.

Despite the infamous events of the past, it was all in good fun and for a good cause. As one of the event officials put it: "Unfortunately, not all history is favorable." And to drive home his point he cited the Hatfields and the McCoys!

In July, 2015, the John Dillinger Museum moved from the Indiana Welcome Center in Hammond to the Old Lake County Courthouse in Crown Point. It would studiously try to portray Dillinger not as a folk hero but the bad guy that he was. The exhibit includes the pants he wore upon the day of his death, a replica of the infamous wooden gun he used for his escape and his "lucky" rabbit's foot. You'll also see a facade of Chicago's old Biograph Threatre where Dillinger was gunned down in its adjacent ally. The theatre screen announces the film, "Manhattan Melodrama," the movie Dillinger saw in his last night on earth. You'll sit in a cracker box jail cell similar to the one in which Dillinger spent nine years and look in on the likes of the gangster's body in the "Lake County Morgue." Add Dillinger's death mask and his original tombstone removed from the Crown Hill Cemetery in Indianapolis after too many people chipped off pieces of it for souvenirs. The message the museum wants to be sure you take away: Crime doesn't pay.

Three of Dillinger's relatives, including a nephew, were on hand at the museum's grand opening to meet visitors, who quickly perceived them harmless.

.

William Revelli directed the University of Michigan band for nearly forty years and raised the standards for college bands nationwide.

Chapter 5:

The Band Plays On

William Revelli led Hobart's school band to four national championships.

William Revelli. His name now hangs over Hobart's bandshell at Festival Park on Lake

George.   Old timers remember him.   A newer resident might ask, "Who was he?"

He came to the Hobart school system in 1924 and began to form its first high school marching band. Two years later he led that band to a national championship as best in the nation.

That was only a start. His band won those same honors for the next three years. Judges included names like Edwin Goldman, Karl King and John Phillip Sousa. By 1934 Revelli's Hobart band had been invited to play at the World's Fair.

Revelli was the son of Italian immigrants. He started as a boy on the violin, riding the train alone from his home in southern Illinois to St. Louis and back every Sunday morning for his lessons. He eventually landed work in the pit orchestra of a large Chicago theatre. The future looked bright to the young musician until the movie industry released its first talking picture, "The Jazz Singer." That killed the pit orchestras almost overnight and hundreds of musicians were suddenly out of work.

Then a family friend told him about the public schools in a small Indiana town called Hobart where he was offered a job as "music supervisor." He took the position but promptly asked if he could start a band. Sure, he was told, "but you'll have no place to rehearse, no funds and no time during the school day for class."

He took the challenge, found rehearsal space in the basement of the Methodist church across the street and went door to door in town to "recover old instruments from attics," even borrowing a drum that he would pick up on a porch in the morning and return in the afternoon.

He inspired band mothers to form a booster club and throw fund raisers serving chicken dinners.

Years later Revelli would remark, "There wasn't a chicken left in Indiana after one of those dinners."

Revelli at first didn't know much about wind and percussion instruments, so for several years he took private lessons, rehearsed with the Chicago Symphony Orchestra and learned to play six instruments. As a southpaw he initially led awkwardly with the baton so colleagues taught him to conduct with his right hand, not left.

At Hobart Revelli was a hard taskmaster who demanded perfection, both on the instruments and on marching style, but when his students weren't scared of him they stood in awe of him. His musicians had to keep their lines straight and smart, the music clear and sharp. He finally left Hobart to direct the University of Michigan's marching band, after first turning down the University of Wisconsin, but he almost didn't take the position because Hobart paid him substantially more than Michigan had offered! But once he accepted, he stayed there for 36 years.

While already a legend in high school ranks, he soon became even more renowned during his years at the University of Michigan. There his band won acclaim for its musical precision, intricate formations and high-stepping style. Said one of his highly-regarded faculty peers, "It's very difficult to talk about Bill Revelli except in superlatives. Nothing ever sounded like a Revelli band but a Revelli band. He was single handedly responsible for raising the standards everywhere, and by his later years he was on a first name basis with the best orchestra leaders in America, including Eugene Ormandy, George Szell and Morton Gould.

Revelli was an innovator. He moved college bands across the country away from rigid military formations. He introduced greater movement and synchronized it with the music. He introduced new music. He also introduced dance steps to his music, the most famous:

Alexander's Ragtime Band. The crowd loved it. In 1949 he introduced the first Band Day at Michigan Stadium with twenty nine high schools attending, but by 1960 the event was drawing more than 40,000 participants. The Buick and Chevrolet divisions of General Motors began to pick up the tab for the band's performance at

away games. At an Ohio State game Revelli decided to show appreciation by lining his band into a Buck-I (Buckeye) formation. Then he moved the I into the center to spell "Buick." How clever, but later Michigan's athletic director reportedly chastised him for mixing the band with commercialism on the football field!

Revelli recruited top musicians like a coach recruits athletes, which gave him a huge band. When in 1969 Michigan hired Bo Schembechler as its football coach, Revelli was the first to visit his office. The two reinforced each other's strong convictions on discipline. Bo urged Revelli to put his men through the paces on the school song, *The Victors.* And so he did. The coach assembled his freshmen in Yost field house. In full uniform Revelli took the podium, tapped his baton, looked the men in the eye and said, "John Philip Sousa called this the greatest fight song ever written. And you will sing it with respect. He blew his pitch pipe, told them how to sing from the diaphragm, and demanded they learn the words. Each fall he repeated the routine with incoming freshmen. The men learned to sing their school song with robust and assurance and, like the band, they perhaps became the "best of their kind in the country."

Frederick C. Ebbs followed Revelli at Hobart (1940-1948). He left to direct the band at Baldwin Wallace, then became Director of the Indiana University bands until his retirement.

More than a decade after the Revelli era my wife played clarinet in the Hobart band under Richard A. Worthington, who later went on to lead the marching bands at the University of Arkansas. After graduation she sold it and has never played since, but I don't think she's never quite gotten the experience out of her blood. On rare occasions, like around the 4th of July, I may catch her marching through our living room to the patriotic music of a CD. Then she'll suddenly halt and make a square turn! Many who once played in a Hobart High School band later joined the "Rusty Pipes," which at first seemed primarily a cluster of Hobart band alumni, but it has long since expanded beyond that. Only recently though did it retire its original name, still beloved by many old timers, and call itself the Hobart Area Concert Band, a classy group of some 50 musicians well regarded in northwest Indiana. In more ways than one today "The Band Plays On," though I've yet to see "Casey waltz with the strawberry blond."

The Hobart Area Concert Band, formerly known as "The Rusty Pipes." Originally comprised primarily of "alumni" from former Hobart High School bands, it is now much broader and has established high respect in northwest Indiana

Abraham Lincoln's hat on exhibit at the Smithsonian Institute in Washington, D.C

The assassination of the President (Getty Images)

Chapter 6:

The Carriage Abe Lincoln Rode to the Ford Theatre

It sits in South Bend and in the movie you can hear the click of its door.

It was another Stephen Spielberg winner, the movie *Lincoln,* released in 2012, which won leading actor Daniel Day-Lewis an Academy Award and grossed more than 275 million dollars at the box office. Sally Field plays Mary Todd Lincoln. The story line focuses on the last four months before Lincoln's assassination as he urges the House of Representatives to pass the Thirteenth Amendment to the U.S. Constitution to abolish slavery before the Civil War actually comes to a close, giving Confederates no chance to frame an armistice that might not include the legislation so critical to the freedom of the black race. This meant he had to persuade enough men from both parties to back the Emancipation Proclamation without further delay. It ultimately passed by just two votes.

In the final scenes of the movie, Lincoln is in conference with his Cabinet when he is reminded that Mrs. Lincoln is waiting to take him to their evening at Ford's Theatre. Son Tad Lincoln is watching *Aladdin and the Wonderful Lamp* at another theatre when a man interrupts to announce that Lincoln has just been shot.

The carriage that transported the Lincolns to the Ford Theatre that night rests in the Studebaker National Museum in South Bend. In the movie, *Lincoln,* you won't see the carriage but you'll hear the click of its door! The movie's sound designer, Ben Burtt, was a stickler for authenticity. When he heard the carriage still existed, he arranged to record the sound of the door's click on site. The museum shut down a

Lincoln's Ford Theatre carriage (Smithonian National Museum of American History)

section of its air conditioning for quiet, and for further sound insulation surrounded the carriage with a blanket. for the 30-minute audio session. It was not the only item Burtt recorded to maintain audio authenticity. He also captured the tick of a Civil War pocket watch Lincoln had used.

As for the carriage itself, the movie directors relied on a reproduction. After Lincoln's death his son Robert Todd Lincoln inherited the historic carriage before it was sold to a doctor F.B. Brewer, who rode in it for years on his medical practice. Then Clement Studebaker bought it, which explains why it wound up in South Bend. In 2006, the Studebaker National Museum received a "Save America's Treasures" grant to conserve its Presidential carriage collection. In that process they discovered that the black carriage had originally been green, with burgundy, gold and white details. They also uncovered elaborate monograms, with the initials A.L. on each door, that had been painted over.

Only days after that fateful night at the Ford Theatre, Lincoln's funeral train rolled into Indiana's Michigan City--nine cars in all with the casket of the nation's 16th President and three hundred mourners and dignitaries aboard.

The train would rumble on to Chicago, then Springfield, on its 1,654-mile journey from Washington, D.C. to the President's final resting place. Throngs had lined the Monon tracks through Westville as women waved flags of mourning trimmed in black crepe and men removed their hats. At Michigan City the train passed under a massive archway of evergreens accented with roses. Ladies of the town had created a huge banner, with one of its messages reading: "With tears we resign thee to God and history." A replica of the Lincoln funeral train was to have rolled into Michigan City May 1, 2015, precisely 100 years after the real event, but because of costs the plans were canceled in lieu of a Lincoln re-enactor.

The Merrillville Historical Society has opened a special exhibit commemorating the Lincoln funeral train and its route through Indiana. It includes a model of the train designed by Hobart historian Dan Kleine. The exhibit will remain through May 1, 2016. "

Barn and granary at the Buckley Homestead
Photo by David Flood

Chapter 7:

Lowell's Buckley Homestead Puts You Back on the Farm

It also takes you back to the way hard-working settlers used to do it.

It's hardly big time corporate farming, with all the high tech today's agri-business relies upon. It's a down-to-earth flashback to the past, a more simple lifestyle yet labor intense.

That's the way you might describe life recreated on a 160-acre piece of property east of

Lowell, now a living history farm but once tilled by an Irish immigrant and his family of four who left Ireland during its devastating potato famine to find a better life in America.

It's a great place to expose children to the rural life of yesteryear while those who might have their grandparents along reminisce about the way they used to do it, or old farm machinery, or quilting or the shed full of antique tools.

Those who take the official tour start at the carriage house and learn about its underground cistern before advancing to the main house and its museum. Many early farms were divided by roads, the farmhouse on one side, barns and shops on the other. On one side the women kept house, tended the garden and handled the chickens. The men worked in the fields and outbuildings on the other. It was a division of labor, somewhat gender driven.

I saw this culture perpetuated in my own childhood days on a California grain ranch. I always wondered as a kid why my uncle never seemed to help my hard working aunt with either the chickens or the garden.

Your Buckley tour takes you next to the old one-room schoolhouse, operative into the 1920s, until the automobile replaced the horse and school districts consolidated. This author too graduated from a one-room school, but the

Your tour of the Buckley pioneer farm includes a look at one of yesteryear's one-room schools. (Photo by David Flood)

shocker is that it's still operational, one of the last of its kind in California. The school is still too isolated from the rest of civilization to close it.

The Buckley school has an outhouse and a water pump. Children are told not to grab the handle too high or they'll pinch themselves.

A path takes you from here along a meandering creek and across a footbridge to a log house built in the 1850s, typical of the kind that housed Indiana's earliest pioneers. You'll also pass a barn, a granary, a milk house, a hog barn and a house for hired hands.

In early days the Buckley barn was loaded to the rafters with hay. Today it houses farm equipment. Hay then was stored loose. Loaded wagons drove under the barn as gigantic hay forks resembling tongs, hanging on ropes guided by pulleys, would come down from the top and lift the hay high for proper stacking. Later farmers began to bale their hay, though it still had to be stacked. And don't bale it too green, or it will heat up later, trigger spontaneous combustion and burn your barn down.

Visitors will find many family attractions at the Buckley homestead with special events often depending upon the season. Look for crafts, family fun, food, concessions, cowboys, music and storytelling. Look also for its annual "Legend of Sleepy Hollow," as a guide escorts visitors through the premises encountering town folk looking for Ichabod Crane, the one person who can tell the stories of the village.

At its fall festival the second weekend of October one might find old fashioned apple dumplings, zucchini relish and kettles of freshly-made soaps. A 4-H club may offer hot dogs and look also for their highly regarded baked potatoes.

Dr. and Mrs. Quackenbush often show up with their quick wit and sleight of hand. Cowboys roam the premises looking for the bad guys and are alert to host riders of the Pony Express. You'll find old fashioned music and dancing at the Pioneer Farm, tall tales at a "Liar's Bench," storytellers at the schoolhouse and even a site where you can pan for gold with the miners.

If you like to throw things, here's your chance. There's a "Sheep Toss," a "Rolling Pin Toss" and a "Frying Pan Toss."

Its annual rustic Yule assembles the atmosphere of "A Christmas Long Ago," and of course you'll enjoy yummies like molasses cookies and cider. And also for the authenticity of yesteryear, you might find an old Sears Roebuck catalog open on the table.

Autumn in the Dunes by South Shore Line.
Artist Ivan V. Beard. Calumet Regional Archives Indiana University Northwest.

Chapter 8:

The Railroad, Poster Art And the Indiana Dunes

Since early days artists have tried to show off America's landscape.

ONE HUNDRED YEARS OF

Enduring Tradition

SOUTH SHORE LINE

It was called the Hudson River School—that fraternity of artists like Thomas Cole and Albert Bierstadt—who painted the Catskills and landscapes of grandeur in the American West. When people in the eastern United States saw these works of art they promptly longed to go there.

In the case of Indiana's lakeshore, it was poster art that first triggered the flow of early day tourism into its woodlands, sand dunes and beaches. Individual posters carried names like *Autumn in the Dunes, Football: Notre Dame, Moonlight in Duneland* and *Just Around the Corner.* When these posters began to appear in Chicago in the 1920s, especially around the South Shore Line, people soon decided they wanted to go there.

Though vintage in style, you can still find these today posted all over northwest Indiana. You can buy them in art galleries, history museums, tourist stops, even the mall. They've become valued collectibles and the art décor for local doctors offices, dentists, hospitals and far more.

Do you call these posters art or illustration? Let's choose both. Norman Rockwell once called the years 1890-1920 the "Golden Age of Illustration." It was the era when art had to sell something. OK, call it advertising too. It came out of commercial art studios. That's not to demean their skills as artists. They had to master the basics and draw well. They also had to know how to work with the process of lithography.

Winter Sports in the Dunes
Artist unknown 1927
(Courtesy Calumet Regional Archives
Indiana University Northwest)

They had to know how to use color and make their landscapes simple but believable.

So why do these posters endure today? Our story starts with the electric powered Lake Shore Line, established in 1901. Population along the line doubled in its first two decades. The line did well in those days, but eventually it began to decline and look shabby, even plagued by debt.

Enter industrial magnate Samuel Insull, an immigrant from England who had been Thomas Edison's private secretary, later an industrialist who owned a broad collection of interurban electric lines, including a very successful one on Chicago's north shore. He saw the potential of northwest Indiana, bought the South Shore line, overhauled the entire system and introduced new passenger cars complete with mahogany interiors.

Insull was also a marketing genius, using colorful brochures, newspaper ads, maps, newsletters and even movies to draw Chicagoans down into northwest Indiana. At the heart of his advertising campaign, though, was the art poster. The illustrations conveyed a climate of fun and relaxation in the Indiana Dunes, showed off its landscapes and even its flora and fauna.

The posters carried the names of several artists, but that of Oscar Hanson perhaps became most prominent. Working from a studio near Chicago's Water Tower, he released in 1927

Winter in the Dunes, Dunes Woodland and *Homeward Bound.* Other artists who frequently contributed to the series included names like Ragan, Brennemann, Huelster and Beard. The posters promoted the lakeshore's beaches, its waters, its trails, its winter sports, Crescent Dunes, Hudson Lake, its four seasons and more. They also promoted its steel mills to stress employment and roamed on down to Notre Dame football at South Bend.

Beaches by the Shore Line
Urgelles, 1925 (Calumet Regional Archives, Indiana University Northwest)

Insull's promotional campaigns worked. The year 1927 became the railroad's glory year. The line was boosted by shuttling Chicagoans on weekend excursions into Indiana. It was not only a strategic blend of train and lake shore recreation, but also a strategy to sell duneland real estate.

Then came the sudden 1929 stock market crash. Freight and passenger service plummeted. The railroad hung on and even continued to give good service. It reduced its run time from Chicago to South Bend to under two hours and won the national *Electric Traction* speed trophy. It still offered dining or parlor car service, but by 1933 it filed bankruptcy. Owner Samuel Insull laid plans to recover.

That was not easy. Insull did not fully foresee the impact the automobile would make on transportation nationwide. Streetcars and electric trains became passé as the government spent billions on new and better roads and highways. General Motors, other automakers and the oil companies lobbied Congress furiously in their own interests, determined to put the electric lines out of business. On a local level the dunes real estate market had all but vanished.

Jump now to the 1970s. Somehow the South Shore Railroad still endured, as if it wanted to be "The Little Train That Could." Commuters rode it daily and it still carried people to Dunesland, but its future appeared uncertain. Pieces were in place to expand the National Lakeshore. The railroad would run through its entire 20-mile length, but a "Save the Dunes" movement gathered steam. Then the South Shore suddenly announced that it might drop its passenger service and carry only freight. Commuters were stunned.

All wanted to save the railroad, but local politicians didn't want to subsidize a privately-owned line owned by CSX. Moreover, why couldn't the railroad make it when at rush hours their cars were jammed? They did not understand that, between the two rush hours of each day, the line was losing big money.

A small ad hoc committee of grass roots residents bolstered by a $5,000 grant and determined to save the railroad, began to "lobby" all the powers that be while also organizing special events to bring folk into northwest Indiana on excursions reminiscent of those "times gone by." It was also timely for them to hear that a part of the dunes lakeshore might soon become a National Park.

Enter once again those old art posters. They had virtually disappeared until a Chicago lawyer stumbled upon a collection of the original posters in a storage locker and delivered them to the owner of a vintage poster shop He restored three of them, re-printed them and offered them for sale. The posters caught on. Eventually the entire series was restored, except for a few forever lost.

By the 1970s it was decided to expand the poster series, with the help of new contributors with names like Flemming, Phillips and Rush. Most prominent has been Mitchell Markovitz, with credentials not only as an award-winning commercial artist but also a locomotive engineer and trainman on the South Shore and other lines.

These vintage posters, with all their nostalgia, continue to sell vigorously, despite the fact that *Autumn in the Dunes* may suggest you can still cruise the dunes by horse and wagon, Notre Dame football helmets are hopelessly outdated and so also is all the beachwear. The top sellers? It's still the two Notre Dame posters, they say, and the flapper girl on the beach with the modest bathing suit and the nice smile.

Meanwhile, the South Shore Line, once labeled "The Little Train That Could," survives. So do the vintage posters that helped to save it.

25 miles of Beach
1925 (lithograph)
Artist: Oscar Rabe Hanson
Calumet Regional Archives
Indiana University Northwest

The Ski Slide at Ogden Dunes

Some called it the largest ski slope structure in the world. The best of Norway once sped down its slopes.
(Ogden Dunes Historical Society).

Chapter 9:

America's Tallest Ski Jump on the Indiana Dunes?

They came from as far as Scandinavia. Some had jumped in the Winter Olympics.

You've got to be kidding. A world class ski jump on the Indiana shores of Lake Michigan? Where are the mountains? Even Mt. Baldy is little more than 300 feet elevation. And on all that sand?

And Olympic jumpers from abroad? This is not Sarejevo, or Innsbruk, nor Lake Placid, or Squaw Valley. Yet the crowds came for five consecutive years (1928-1932). Ten thousand, they say, perhaps more.

OK, so while they chose to jump from a steep slope in Ogden Dunes, that height alone wasn't enough, so on top they built a towering metal framework that stretched on upward nearly another 200 feet from its base on the back side, but they first dynamited the sand to reach a solid foundation. Skiers had to ascend a long flight of stairs to the starting gate.

It was billed as "the largest artificial ski jump structure in America," its height equal to

Emil Biorn 1927 (Calumet Regional
Archives, Indiana University Northwest)

that of a 22-story building. Built of steel, it was a
natural for the region, with U.S. Steel anchoring
the shoreline only a few miles to the west. Skiers
could attain speeds up to 75 miles an hour at take-
off. The South Shore Railroad stood ready to sell
thousands of tickets, citing the fact that Chicago
area Scandinavians numbered 123,000.

Down its slope came the best of Norway: Birger Ruud, Hans Beck and Kaare Wahlberg. All three would jump in the 1932 Winter Olympics, which Norway swept. The longest jump recorded at the dunes during these years: 195 feet, a strong show but not quite reaching Canadian Nels Nelson's record of 212 feet.

The initial event in 1928 was not without incident. Dry grass caught fire from a carelessly discarded cigarette. Scores of parked cars were scorched, two badly damaged. Snowfall often came up short. In the event's final year snow was imported from Gavitz, Wisconsin. The Norwegians showed up once more, in part because a week earlier the conditions they had encountered at Lake Placid were even worse. Strong northwest winds that year prompted a number of spills, with 22-year old Gunnar Oman of Ogden Dunes among its victims and the gusts probably prevented an expected new record.

It was the Ogden Dunes Ski Club (originally called the Grand Beach Ski Club) that initiated this grand project. Visionaries saw how they could take advantage of a sandy slope and also sell real estate around its perimeters, much like a golf course.

Though at first a success, it soon fell on hard times. Enter the 1929 stock market crash. Then years of short snowfall. The hill was hard to climb.   And it was difficult to collect the admissions. It held its last event in 1932. Two years later the structure was dismantled and sold to the town of Rockford, Illinois.

These ski jump events were international, so for a half decade, at least, Indiana's unique winter sports venue drew world attention. Its promotion was enhanced by one of the early South Shore posters and also by film footage taken to impress people far and wide of the gigantic ski structure, the beauty of Lake Michigan and its dunes.

When the Lake Michigan shoreline lost its only ski jump, local enthusiasts had to shift to such sites as the Norge Ski Jump in River Grove northwest of Chicago, built in 1905. The Norge Ski Club is now the oldest ski club in America. Michigan's Hanson Hills was built in 1929. Today's fastest-growing winter sport, however, is snowboarding, which is about to overtake skiing.

In 1936, three years after the closure of the Ogden Dunes slide, the annual Chicago ski jump tournament built a gigantic steel slide over the top of the Soldier Field grandstand, only to have a snowstorm prevent its use on the day of the great event. It had to settle for a smaller slide built outside the field's south end. The next year the weather cooperated. An international ski jump was also held over Wrigley Field in 1944.

While the Ogden Dunes ski jump is long gone, Indiana's dunes still attract its share of winter sports enthusiasts, especially for cross-country skiing, sledding, snowshoeing. Click on the Indiana Dunes Tourism's webpage and you'll find miles of trails, but bring your own skis. For local cross country, many suggest Talltree Arboretum, Sunset Hill Farm County Park in Valparaiso, Coffee Creek Watershed Preserve in Chesterton, the Dunes State Park and the Indiana Dunes National Lakeshore Glenwood Dunes and Tolleston Dunes. Check out also where you can ice skate and ice fish.

Has history left any evidence of the lakeshore's once grand ski jump event? Yes, there's a plaque planted in 1997 authorized by the Ogden Dunes Historical Society—at Boat Club Road where Kratz Field is located today and where the jump once stood. You can even enjoy a visual tour of a home that sits atop the hill once a world class ski jump by clicking on to You Tube and 15 Ski Hill Road.

You can also visit the Ogden Dunes Historical Society where docents will bring out old film footage of this event's ski jump action and you can "re-live" the event's glory days when thousands once gathered to see Alpine-style ski jumping on the Indiana sands.

Yesteryear is just around the corner.

Hobart ducks could protest with an upside down flyover akin to the acrobatics of the Gary Air Show but they don't really want to quack up.

Plastic ducks like those in Hobart's annual dam duck race are a laugh, some say. They're imposters.
Will the real ducks please stand up!

It's a crowded field but somewhere are winners.

Chapter 10:

Walt Disney, Lake George and the Real Hobart Duck

It happened one recent year in May. Mother Duck proudly paraded her ten chicks down Hobart's 10th St. Her big flat web feet crossed a storm drain with ease, but four ducklings following behind her tumbled through the grate into murky waters ten feet below.   .

Horrified onlookers rushed to the rescue,

including the Hobart Police Department, ready to "serve and protect." The Street Department released the grate. The ducklings were saved Everyone cheered..

Said an official afterwards, "Hobart loves its ducks."

Families regularly stroll Hobart's lakefront to feed them cracked corn and bread. Each morning and evening tax consultant Pam Mellon, who lives on the northwest edge of Lake George, turns her sidewalk into an outdoor lakefront duck restaurant. Up to fifty customers can show up.

The city touts its annual "Dam Duck Race" held each August. It's a family event so they censor out the "n." It's impossible to bleep it.

The duck race fundraiser concludes Hobart's four-day Lakefront Festival. Officials dump thousands of plastic ducks over the dam at Lake George. A $5 raffle ticket gets you one duck, each duck numbered. The ducks drift slowly so enablers with paddle sticks on shore and in canoes help them along. The winning duck earns his sponsor a thousand dollars.

The whole event is impressive, but the ducks are imposters. Real ducks waddling the shore or flying overhead could be insulted. They could protest with an upside down flyover, but ducks don't like to quack up. My apologies. Now for the kids they've added cardboard boat races

Entries are held together by duct tape. A mis-use of the bird's name? Ducks hope it doesn't stick.

If the Hobart Brickies in an earlier year had not adopted Yohan Petrovich as their mascot, I believe, it would have been a duck. Duck Creek even flows underneath its south bleachers.

My wife and I live off Hwy 51 in Hobart's Laurawood opposite Sapper's nursery. Our home backs up to wooded wetlands and at one time our street had adopted its own pair of resident ducks. They came back year after year.

How did we know they were the same ducks? The female had a limp. I labeled them Maggie and Jiggs, which harks back to an old comic strip that will surely date me. One morning Jiggs waited on our front walk, looking intently up and down the street for about ten minutes. He at first looked worried, impatient, then disgusted. Suddenly, Maggie flew in from the west at full speed. Jiggs flapped his wings and flew up to join her on her descent in a graceful curve and with perfect side by side timing that suggested they might be rehearsing for the Gary Air Show. They both splash landed in the wetlands behind us.

My wife quipped, "Jiggs probably thinks Maggie spent too long at the mall." But she still had her drab wardrobe. Jiggs looked in sharp style as if he'd just left the Men's Warehouse. He liked the way he looked.

So recently I got to thinking why ducks are so lovable. First I paid tribute to Walt Disney, who more than 75 years ago introduced Donald Duck in the movie, *The Wise Little Hen.* Everyone adores this duck despite the fact he's easily annoyed and has an explosive temper.

More level headed Daisy Duck has to quiet him down. Disney also created Micky Mouse, an almost perfect example of good behavior, but when my wife sees a mouse, she screams and I head to the hardware for a mouse trap. It's the only way we'll feed a mouse cheese.

So we'll dismiss the Disney theory. Ducks are just naturally funny. They waddle on land but why do they fly so fast and walk so slow?

Our local ducks can stand on their heads to eat. Their ability to duck into the water for food ties to the entomology of their very name. Other ducks hang out in deeper waters and dive for their food without scuba gear. Ducks are social. That's why they group en masse on Lake George. These ducks belong to the quack pack. Some ducks, like Maggie and Jiggs, prefer to hang out in a more quiet pond like the one behind our house. It's

Hobart ducks know welfare when they see it. (Photo by David Flood)

their private jacuzzi. When a neighbor across the street first discovered Maggie had nested in his backyard bushes, the mother was already parading her chicks off his premises, obviously proud of her duck dynasty. He couldn't believe it so he called the previous owner, who had moved to Las Vegas.

"Yeah, they come back there every year," the earlier owner confirmed. Why didn't she nest in the wetlands? Our neighbor had a small pool.

Lake George has long been a stopover for migrating ducks and geese, but for some of them

Hobart was not always their "hometown," so we're told. Decades ago residents started to release pet Easter ducks into the pond north of the dam once they got too big. The town began to collect cash in canisters to feed them.

Migratory ducks knew welfare when they saw it. They settled in among the rocks north of the dam--let's call it "Ellis Island"--and hung around long enough to assure their Lake George citizenship papers. Over time they forgot their migratory flight path. Today some of these ducks have no high tech GPS savvy to figure out how to proceed on south.

Travis Castilleja, longtime Lake George angler who works at the Hobart Bait Shop, believes Hobart's well meaning "duckatarians" altered the natural order. Today's Lake George ducks have even settled into their own neighborhoods: the bridge and dam ducks, the bayou ducks, the Wisconsin Street ducks.

Ducks have to be athletic. They play football in Oregon and hockey in Anaheim. In the Quad Cities the Mallards play minor league baseball. When the bases are loaded, sportscasters will tell you there are "three ducks on the pond." My apologies once again.

Philatelists value duck stamps, but proud ducks don't know the stamp is not for postage. It's a hunting license for their demise. Donald Duck and his Disney companions can be found on U.S. postage and on postal stamps from scores of other nations, making him the premier world traveler and the airline industry's most frequent flyer.

You can find duck cartoons on the internet. Maggie and Jiggs have motivated my research on ducks. Farm ducks, I learned, don't fly, or at least very high or very far. They're clumsy. The Wright Brothers flew better at Kitty Hawk. They are descendants of the Peking duck domesticated centuries ago by the Chinese. Another product made in China!

Most ducks simply quack, but some make other sounds and one kind, they say, can even yodel. I've yet to meet Cowboy Duck..

Tragedy can easily surround the duck. Racoons can quickly turn duck eggs into an omelette. Consider terms like "dead duck" and "duck soup." And no duck likes the phrase, "getting all your ducks in a row."

Not long ago a speeding motorist ran down a mother duck in front of Sapper's Nursery. It looked deliberate There's a steep fine for that. Onlookers were furious. I accidentally almost clipped Jiggs in the twilight one evening, turning into our drive. "I would have been crushed," I said in anguish to my passenger friend beside me.

"Not to mention the duck," he quipped.

Del Mundy, an authority on Hobart ducks who won the Indiana state duck calling contest back in 1964, told me a duck had once nested atop the town's Chase Bank, choosing to deposit her nest eggs on the bank's roof rather than in a savings account. When it came time for her chicks to fly, she stood below and ordered them one by one-- each with a quack--to push off Bank customers protecting their own nest eggs stood by with high interest. Ma Duck then bid her landlord adieu.

Only hours before I had interviewed Dale, a neighbor had given him a huge stuffed duck her kids had outgrown. He took it to Hobart's Bright Spot Restaurant that morning, sat it in the seat beside him and became the talk of the day. Before he left the cafe he gave it to a wide-eyed child.

This may be all you want to know about ducks. If not, go to their website. Repeat. Footnote: "Website."

The pier head lighthouse at Michigan City

Chapter 11:

Indiana's Lighthouse and Shipwreck History

Did a landlocked state need a "big lantern" to warn the ships at sea?

Light houses. You'll find them along the Atlantic from its southeastern shores to the rockbound coast of Maine and along the U.S. rim of the Pacific. But in Indiana?

Yes, locals know there's a lake out there and Indiana has a 45-mile coast line, but those anchored outside the Midwest can sometimes be caught by surprise. Upon her plane's approach to Chicago on a flight from New York to San Francisco my California cousin suddenly looked down upon the waters of Lake Michigan and feared she had boarded the wrong plane. She fared better than the West Coast flyer who thought he'd boarded a flight for Oakland until he looked down out over Pacific waters and the pilot announced the plane was headed for Aukland, New Zealand. True story.

It can also surprise people that the U.S. Coast Guard was founded not on one of our great ocean shores but in Grand Haven, Michigan. The rim of the Great Lakes still has its own array of historic lighthouses.

Indiana has just one. It goes back to 1837 when the U.S. Government established a lighthouse at Michigan City (the town is in Indiana, though hugging the Michigan border.) It was little more than a post lamp on a rather low-level whitewashed tower with an over-sized light on top, its mission to guide ships into the town's port. It was replaced in 1858 by another lighthouse, which still stands today, converted into the Michigan City Lighthouse Museum. Its lantern at first burned lard oil, though it would congeal in the cold and fog the lens with soot. Whale oil did OK but with the decline of the American whaling industry it was cheaper to use kerosene.

At the outset of the Civil War Harriet Colfax, cousin to Abraham Lincoln's Vice President, Schuyler Colfax, was appointed lighthouse keeper. She had taught school, voice and piano. Along with a companion, Ann Hartwell, she handled that job for more than forty years. In 1871 the government installed its first beacon light, mounted at the east pier head and accessible only by a 1,500-foot elevated catwalk. The light keeper had to climb to the lanterns twice each evening to trim the wick, polish the lens and refuel.

Authorities later shifted the light to the west side of Trail Creek and positioned it 500 feet further out into the lake. Miss Colfax would have to row across Trail Creek and cross the catwalk to deliver the fuel. Envision all of these precarious maneuvers in icy conditions and a fierce storm. Records document many tales of heroism and the keepers were so good at the job that Great Lakes seamen dubbed Indiana's lighthouse "Old Faithful." The lighthouse at first operated only April-November but later extended its watch to year round.

Keepers lived in the 1858 lighthouse. In 1904 the structure was remodeled to accommodate, when needed, four duplex apartments. In 1939 the U.S. Coast Guard took command, after which the 1858 structure stood vacant for a quarter century, suffering neglect and vandalism until restored and converted to the museum visitors can enjoy today. Here you can climb the tower into the lantern room, examine the Fresnel lens that once illuminated lake waters, learn about Lake Michigan's shipwrecks, read about the stop of Abraham Lincoln's funeral train in Michigan City and see a display of running lights from the ship *Showboat*.

Lighthouses on Lake Michigan have surely prevented many disasters, but these waters still hold more shipwrecks than once thought. Some of them have been dramatically revealed by aerial photography, especially when lake waters drop or when the waters are unusually clear. Underwater archaeologists continue to document these relics, like that of the *Muskegon,* which went down in 1910, and the *J.D. Marshall,* which sank in 1911. Four men died. The *Marshall's* massive three-bladed cast iron propeller is housed at the Indiana Dunes State Park.

Archaeologists have also documented the remains of the *David Dows*, the only five-mast schooner to have navigated the Great Lakes, and the *Wheeler*, a steam freighter that broke in half and sank in 1893. Over time the value of some relics still under water has been compromised by looters and vandals, who not only risk their own lives but also imprisonment.

No ship disaster was more tragic, though, than that of the *USS Eastland.* It was July 24, 1915, when 2,501 employees of Western Electric boarded the ship in Chicago for an anticipated gala company picnic in Michigan City. Thousands of others (seven thousand tickets were sold) stood ready to board other steamers—including the *Theodore Roosevelt* and the *Petoskey.* Families waited with picnic baskets loaded, eager to enjoy the festivities ahead. When the ship had fully loaded,

The USS Eastland with 2,500 passengers aboard prepares to depart for a gala picnic in Michigan City, Indiana, many waving from both ashore and from the top. No one at that moment could have foreseen the disaster that was about to happen. (Photo courtesy the Associated Press Archives)

dockworkers brought in the gangplank. Those still waiting on the riverbank waved enthusiastically at those on board high above. The lucky ones, they thought. First out.

In the ship's ballroom the orchestra struck up the music. Some began to dance, unaware that the ship had already begun to list a bit. Then back. Some joked about the uneven dance floor. Chairs slowly slid across the deck. The mood suddenly turned somber when the engines stopped and beer bottles tumbled from the counters. The orchestra belted out an upbeat ragtime, but by now panic had set in. Rogue pianos, ice boxes and furniture tumbled onto some passengers, killing them instantly. Frantic passengers with children in arms emerged from the lower decks. Some passengers began to leap into the river and swim toward the pier. The ship's tilt soon reached breaking point. The *USS Eastland* rolled on its side, like a huge whale ready to take a nap, throwing hundreds into the water and trapping further hundreds underneath. Horrified bystanders threw wooden crates and whatever they could grab into the water to help the thrashing multitudes reach shore. A tugboat quickly pulled in alongside and tried to transfer those fortunate enough to be standing by now on the prone ship's upper side.

It was a bright sunny day. No wind. No storm. The waters calm, a complete contrast to the fierce elements surrounding the sinking of the *Titanic,* but though it all happened so quickly, one saw the same kind of terror and it ended in the same kind of tragedy. Most were in tears, some hysterical. A total of 844 passengers and crew died. The horrific event still stands by far as the largest loss of life from a single shipwreck on the Great Lakes. Twenty two entire families were lost. With so many children aboard, the average age of the victims was 23.

George Halas, who would go on to found the Chicago Bears football club, was to have been on the *USS Eastland*, but he overslept. Latecomers arriving to board one of the boats to follow the picnic's flagship heard someone with a megaphone announce "Western Electric picnic called off." They expressed great disappointment until they soon learned why.

At Indiana's Michigan City earlier that July morning the town had prepared for the massive picnic it would host at popular Washington Park Beach for the jubilant crowd expected to arrive in port. It was not to be. Instead, the entire nation joined the city in mourning.

There is sad irony to the story. The *Titanic* had sunk in the Atlantic only three years earlier, the rescue of passengers hampered by a shortage of life boats. New government law soon required that all passenger liners and excursion ships carry lifeboats for all. The ship began to list, some say, when too many passengers shifted to one side, but the weight of the extra lifeboats, it was later speculated, may have been the final straw.

The angry public gathered demanding answers. One man even punched the captain in the nose. Many of the ship's crew were soon arrested but workers had done nothing criminal. It was a company whitewash. It had been known much earlier, however, that the *USS Eastland* had a bad record and basic design flaws. It was top heavy. Its ballast tanks were slow. Owners had tried to solve their problems with a band aid approach. Then to accommodate the new lifeboat law, they had poured another ten tons of concrete into its deck, raising the center of gravity.

Despite the magnitude of the tragedy and the ongoing suffering of those who had lost family and friends, the story soon faded. These were working class folk, many of them recent immigrants. There was no John Jacob Astor aboard. Or other prominent notables. A week after the tragedy in nearby Michigan a millionaire heiress was married. That story drew more press coverage than did the *USS Eastland.*

So blame corporate corruption? The company workforce? The press? A fickle public unaware of its own bias and enamored by the celebrity culture? It's not a new question.

Though much of this tragic story may have been buried for a full century, the *Chicago Tribune* only months before the event's recent anniversary uncovered in a dimly-lit basement archive five floors below Michigan Avenue more than one hundred glass-plate negatives capturing the disaster in close-up. These were taken long before most photography could record breaking news, both because of expense and the time needed in that journalistic era for photo processing. It was a timely find for a story that, in some sense, had long been submerged.

In Michigan City on July 25, 2015, one hundred years after the disaster, several hundred gathered to remember the victims of this tragedy. The event was organized by the Michigan City Historical Society and the Old Lighthouse Eastland Disaster Memorial. Tour guides, two new bronze plaques, museum artifacts and selected documents helped tell the story. A 265-foot stud anchor chain lined the route to the Trail Creek wharf, where the *USS Eastland* was to have docked for the gigantic picnic on Lake Michigan's southeastern shore that never happened. The ceremony ended with a gun salute and the playing of taps.

The ceremony was staged exactly at the hour the *USS Eastland* was to have arrived in Michigan City one hundred years earlier with its boatloads of festive picnickers. How many links in the chain that escorted these folk? Exactly 844, the number of lives lost that day.

History is still around the corner.

(Photo by Greg Hauport)

The Waukeusa Dime Store recently opened a new store in Granger, Indiana.

Chapter 12:

Scouting Old Fashioned Candy Counters

From hard candies to chocolates to gummies, all ages keep in the hunt.

Some time back a group of older folk up in Grayslake, Illinois, decided to meet on a regular schedule just to reminisce. But each time the topic would be pre-defined. It might be their days in 4-H. It might be Christmas memories. Or on at least one occasion: candy.

Like music, candies can even define an era, or a decade, as did vaudeville, or the Charleston, or swing music, or the jitterbug. As these folk reminisced about their favorite candies they probably tipped off their era of childhood.

My grandparents whose childhoods spanned the turn of the last century, talked more about hard candy than chocolates, and if some of it, along with an orange, wound up in their Christmas stockings they seemed satisfied. Hard candy must have still dominated into the 20s, when an old time vocalist called "Haywire Mac" made popular his song, *The Big Rock Candy Mountains*. Its lyrics seemed to suggest that his rock candy mountain was little short of paradise.

It seems the "history" of candy goes back even to Christopher Columbus, who brought chocolate back from the West Indies, though he didn't care much for its bitter sweet taste. Spain took another taste and a decade later decided it had potential.

Whitman's chocolates go back to 1854, Thompson's chocolates to the 1880s. Chocolate imported from Germany caught the attention of Milton Hershey at the 1893 Chicago Columbian Exposition and by the next year in Pennsylvania he had produced the first Hershey bar and even added almonds.

Neccos, those candy discs of assorted flavors and colors, emerged in 1901, long one of my favorites. But at a CVS pharmacy not long ago I couldn't find them, so I asked the girl at the register. She gave me a blank stare. She'd never heard of them.

Life Savers hit the market in 1912. Again recently I realized, incredulously, that those little

The South Bend Chocolate Company has three outlets in South Bend , including a cafe, also one in Valparaiso and one in Indianapolis.

tubes of spearmint, peppermint and wintergreen had almost vanished. No, not so, they said, but you now often have to buy them by the bag. How could a candy with so much seniority, I thought, have been so unceremoniously semi-retired?

Well, with the 1920s came Fannie May Candies, O Henry, Reese's Peanut Butter Cups and Baby Ruth, named not after the famous slugger but for President Grover Cleveland's daughter Ruth, born in a earlier era. Then followed Mounds, Milky Way, Hershey's Kisses, Mr. Goodbar, Milk Duds and Heath Bars.

The 1930s brought Tootsie Rolls and 3Musketeers, the 1940s M&M Plain chocolate. Many of these choices still survive, though others have disappeared from the mainstream. Look hard, though, and you may still find them. The term for them today seems to be "retro-candy."

Search the internet and you'll find websites that let you order these candies on line, but that doesn't give you the real feel of an old time candy store. So wander out to places like the Wakarusa Dime Store or the South Bend Chocolate Factory or the candy corner at Designer Desserts, the latter two both in Valparaiso. Don't miss the Candy Cove in Crown Point's Old Courthouse Square, which calls itself

Hobart's Albanese Candy near Merrillville is one of northwest Indiana's most popular destinations and you can also enjoy a great tour of its sprawling factory, choice of guided or self guided. Its gummies are sold around the world.

"the sweetest destination." So click on "candy northwest Indiana" on the internet and you'll find more candy stores, including several in Elkhart.

Just about everyone , though, will also look to the region's own Albanese Candy Factory on Rt. 30, which specializes in gummies but also carries a full selection of chocolates and old fashioned candies that have disappeared from the mainstream. It is a real Willy Wonka chocolate factory, though it has shut off the chocolate waterfall that once fascinated customers.

The place has the feel of an old-fashioned candy shop, though it hardly fits a small town setting, with its huge factory and warehouse behind the candy shop itself that seems to stretch half way to Indianapolis. It was founded only in 1983, which hardly makes it a vintage company, but with gummies it has pioneered on the cutting edge and today it sells to a worldwide market. It is truly one of the area's most attractive enterprises, drawing customers from afar. It is also the only producer of gummies in the nation that offers daily tours of its factory, with the options of a personal tour or a self-guided one.

Oh, there's also gum. Names like Blackjack, Clove and Beeman's. William Wrigley introduced his juicy fruit flavor in 1893. It was an experiment. Pardon, Spearmint. By gummit!

Photo courtesy Candy crate.com

The Story of Rock Candy

Rock candy's history goes back centuries. Persian poets mentioned it. It was widely regarded to have both therapeutic and preservative values. Shakespeare in Henry IV (1596) referred to its therapeutic value as a throat soother for long winded talkers.

It even found its way into America's musical folklore. During the 1920s hobo singer "Haywire Mac" McClintock (left) recorded his song, *The Big Rock Candy Mountains.*

He invited folks along to a land of milk and honey where drifters never had to labor, "where they hung the jerk that invented work," where handouts grew on bushes, a land of lemonade springs and "cigarette trees". the latter a phrase folk singer Burl Ives would later change to "peppermint trees" to fit an audience of children. The original recording by "Haywire Mac" became embedded in the soundtrack of the Oscar-nominated movie, *Where Art Thou, Oh Brother?* starring George Clooney.

Associated Press Wikipedia

Dale Messick at the drawing boards in 1953.
(Associated Press Wikipedia)

Chapter 13:

Cartoonist Dale Messick: Brenda Starr Reporter

She first revealed her skills at Hobart High School but later her pioneer comic strip would reach millions.

If you read the comics as a kid, as most of us did, who did you follow? Let me guess: Dick Tracy? Red Ryder? Alley Oop? Chic Young's Blondie (Dagwood)? Nancy (remember Sluggo)? Bringing Up Father (Maggie and Jiggs)? You say, " Jiggs?" Who's he? Alley who? OK, let's skip to a later generation and try Peanuts or Garfield the cat. They're still around, long running and very popular. Now you may have passed over reporter Brenda Starr, but millions of others did not.

Brenda Starr's episodes as a journalist were filled with adventure and romance. At its peak in the 1950s *Brenda Starr Reporter* ran in 250 newspapers and its creator had established herself as the first woman cartoonist to be syndicated.

She was not the first woman illustrator. By the turn of the century male editors who dominated the industry had conceded that advertising people at least needed women to help illustrate such items as Jell-O, soup and baby products. But a woman cartoonist? And her protagonist was an aggressive freewheeling female journalist and investigator on the snoop long before Angela Lansbury on *Murder She Wrote?* Or Mary Richards (Mary Tyler Moore) and her editor, Lou Grant (Ed Asner). Or tough female television journalist Murphy Brown (Candice Bergen). The concept was a hard sell in those earlier days.

Messick was born in South Bend in 1906, the daughter of a sign painter, from whom she got her early interest in art. Her mother was a  seamstress, who may have first planted her daughter's interest in fashion. The family moved to Hobart, Indiana, where Messick was soon drawing scenes for her classmates while only in the seventh grade. At Hobart's high school (senior photo at left) she cranked out a heavy amount of art for its yearbook, *Aurora,* and got better by the year. On a division page introducing the faculty her art gently poked fun at some of the teachers. She found school somewhat dull. She was left handed, near-sighted and couldn't read the schoolroom clock.

After high school she studied commercial art, hired on with engraving companies and greeting card firms and worked on her comic strip at night. When a publisher rejected her first submission, she was devastated. It was called *Steamline Babies,* featuring two young women pursuing fame and fortune in New York. The editors favored a strip based on a radio play of Charlie McCarthy and Edgar Bergen,

Messick got her big break with the *Chicago Tribune-New York News* syndicate, though at first editors preferred simply to take her to lunch but not regard her work seriously. The editors finally accepted *Brenda Starr, Reporter,* though it would not have happened had not the newspaper syndicate's top secretary pulled her strip from an office trash can, suggested some changes and advised Messick to change her name from Dalia to Dale, a clever end run around the sexism she faced.

The newspaper syndicate liked the strip's blend of adventure, fashion and romance, despite the fact her protagonist would invade a journalistic world then dominated by men. It gave it a go. A decade later her comic strip was read by millions. Whether kidnapped, near death on a ski slope or hijacked on the high seas, she would survive nearly as many close calls as Indiana Jones. Unlike Superman's Lois Lane, Brenda Starr could solve her own problems and get out of her own fixes.

Messick borrowed the name Brenda Starr from a debutante of the 1930s and gave her the appearance of Rita Hayworth. She had grown up in the flamboyant flapper age and been hit by the depression. She settled into her professional field at the beginning of World War II and the emergence of Rosie the Riveter. Her occupational choice of reporter for Brenda allowed her protagonist to travel the world to find glamour and adventure.

Brenda Starr, Messick often admitted, was her alter ego. The strip allowed her to sass her editor at *Flash* newspaper and file stories late. Like Messick, Brenda had red hair. She even named her own daughter Starr.

When her protagonist married the mysterious Basil St. John in 1976, President Gerald Ford sent the two a congratulatory telegram. The groom had an eye patch and an undefined ailment that could only be helped by a serum derived from black orchids imported from the Amazon. No such orchid, of course, really existed.

She was especially fond of Paris. There one story line reveals that her mysterious husband Basil St. John was helping train teachers in the repressive land of "Kazookistan," at risk to his life. Later Messick moved reporter Starr to India and then to Belize in Central America, pursuing a story on political corruption. At a holiday newspaper party on January 2, 2011, Starr announced her retirement. There she said her good-byes and left teary-eyed. Brenda Starr, reporter, retired from the scene after more than a half century. Only a few months earlier the industry had also retired the long-running comic strip, *Little Orphan Annie.*

Over the years Messick's work reflected certain fashion trends and she even tried to set some of her own. When she dyed her poodle pink, the craze caught on across the country. She often emphasized long noses and false eyelashes.

When Messick's earliest version of Brenda Starr first appeared decades ago, her four brothers promptly sent her an alert that Brenda needed to be more curvaceous. Messick obliged. A sailor, noting the change, sent a request that she make Brenda even more "daring." Messick sent him a drawing of Brenda tumbling over Niagara Falls in a barrel!

In 1952 the cartoonist moved back to northwest Indiana, specifically Ogden Dunes, where she lived until 1968. She worked out of her own studio at 43 Shore Drive near the lake at a time when the conflict between the South Shore industrial complex and forces to "Save the Dunes" reached high crescendo. At one point in her story line Messick introduced a flashy nightclub run by one "Burns Ditch" that she positioned across from "Villa Bay Shores Estates." One unhappy newspaper columnist saw it as a thinly veiled political slam against U.S. Steel. Messick married and divorced twice.

Actress Joan Woodbury plays "Brenda Starr: Reporter," in the 1945 Columbia movie by that name. Though it's a cliffhanger, her inept "cart-before-the-horse" newspaper copy boy, Pesky, played by William "Billy" Benedict (center), repeatedly bumbles her verbal instructions but eventually comes out a hero. The actor at right is Syd Saylor. (Photo Associated Press Archives).

In 1980 she retired as the strip's illustrator and did only the story line. Several have handled the art since, including *Chicago Tribune's* Mary Schmich, she also a local columnist for the *Post Tribune.* Some critics felt Messick's successors did not maintain Brenda's original glamour and fashion. Newspapers in recent years have downsized the dimensions of their comic strips, which limits the artist's "elbow room" and the graphic impact of a "soap opera" type strip.

If you want to know if people are really reading your strip, she once said, make a mistake. She once drew a cast on a figure's leg, then in a following frame inadvertently drew it on his other leg. She was deluged with letters from those who had caught it.

In 1995 Brenda Starr was honored in a commemorative comic strip series of 20 U.S. postage stamps. Among all their creators, only Dale Messick at the time was still living. She died in Oregon in 2005.

If you want to see firsthand her artwork in Hobart yearbooks, simply drop in to the Hobart Historical Society (across from "Brickie Bowl") on any Saturday morning.

Yesteryear is just around the corner.

The Society for the Preservation and Encouragement of Barbershop Quartet Singing in America

OLD MILL STREAM

The 1991 Top-20 Barbershop Quartets

Chapter 14:

Looking for Yesteryear
Down by the Old Mill Stream

Did an old mill in Lake County
inspire a famous barber shop song?

Wander through the Hobart Historical Society just north of old Brickie Bowl and you'll find a vintage piano that, at one time at least, displayed the sheet music of the barber shop classic, *Down by the Old Mill Stream.* In its time one could say that it was a melody certainly in that era's "mainstream." Sorry.

The music was placed prominently on that piano for a reason, backed by a story of the past that suggested the song might have been inspired by a Hobart millstream setting.

The evidence, however, seems to document a different origin of this song. It was written in 1908, says an official source, by one Tell Taylor, whose friends did not think it of commercial value. Two years later he published it anyway, and when a vaudeville quartet sang it at a Woolworth store in Kansas City, Taylor sold more than a thousand copies of the sheet music he'd brought along. In today's technology it would have probably gone viral on You Tube!

It would be easy to imagine such legend, whether the waterwheel at the old grist mill in Deep River Park, still in existence, or the one that once powered George Earle's lumber mill at the dam on Lake George. Some nice sweet young couple of that era might have been strolling around Hobart's lakeshore, later inspired to remind his girl in song that it was there "I first met you."

The record album, *Down by the Old Mill Stream,* shown on the previous page and released in 1991, can be ordered by clicking *www.allmedia.com.*

The water wheel at Deep River Park in Hobart.
Photograph by David Flood

If the legend were firmly documented, and the mill still stood, imagine the tourism it might draw! It could have been like "the little brown church in the vale" in Nashua, Iowa, which attracts several thousand visitors each year. Maybe the Hobart Chamber of Commerce should try some revisionist history, but that wouldn't be honest. So the town settles for the crowds the pond draws for its annual Dam Duck Race.

The most we can say is that in 1845 Englishman George Earle did construct a dam to power a sawmill and gristmill, created a millpond and in the process backed up Deep River, which in turn created a land of bayous. Today Hobart enjoys a beautiful lakefront, which can still lend itself to a romantic stroll, water tumbling over into Earle's pond, but no longer with his mill. It burned to the ground in 1953.

So perhaps we can discount the song's alleged Hobart connection, but all this should not overlook the grist mill at Deep River, which most certainly has become a point of romance, with the surrounding beauty of the landscape and an adjacent gazebo that each year hosts a full schedule of weekend weddings.

My wife had a cousin married there one summer, the last of five scheduled for a Saturday afternoon. As our wedding crowd gathered, clouds began to blacken and distant thunder moved ever so closer. Only minutes into the wedding ceremony the heavens opened, and all of us had to take cover under the gazebo. Though it was an untimely downpour and the bride got drenched, it was a wedding no one ever forgot!

It was 1835 when John Wood of Massachusetts headed West to the frontier, looking for the right site for a grist mill that would make him good money. He found it along Indiana's Deep River, thanks to a treaty between the United States and the Potawatomi Indians that would permit him to buy land. He paid $200 for 160 acres, cut lumber to build his grist mill and had it up and running by 1838, the first industry in Northwest Indiana. Today it's all a part of Deep River Park, more than a thousand acres which stretch across Hwy 30 to take in also the tremendously popular Deep River Water Park, all of this owned by the county.

In season visitors can check in at park headquarters, once an old church built in 1904. It includes a gift shop, and you'll usually find its volunteers in vintage clothing. You're sure you've stepped back into yesteryear.

By request they'll probably show you how to grind corn, its heavy grist stones crunching the kernels underneath, though the mill today is powered by a motor, not water. The mill had fallen into disrepair, and for more than 45 years it had been closed down altogether. Visionaries restored it, once they found an old mill in Virginia, dismantled its heavy mechanisms and trucked it to Indiana, only to find that originally it had been made in Indianapolis!

Here schoolteacher and volunteer David Gunnerson likes to show schoolchildren how to grind corn. "They want to see that yellow corn coming down the chute into the bucket," he told *The Beacher* weekly magazine. "Some of the younger kids come with the notion that I'm going to send corn flakes down the chute!"

The kids also learn that John Wood created a community around this store, which included a blacksmith shop, shoe shop, cider mill, cheese factory and an ice cream house.

Records also say that when engineers, generally following the old Sauk Indian trail, surveyed the course of Rt. 30, the outpost's owner at that time had enough clout with authorities to assure that they would divert the road a bit to let it pass directly in front of his store.

Beaver felt hats, the fashion style in
Europe and the eastern United States,
created a demand for beaver pelts. This
demand, and the Potawatomi Indians'
desire for trade items such as blankets,
knives, metal hatchets, fabric and
clothing, enabled Joseph Bailly to
operate a modest fur trading business
in the 1820's. Potawatomis brought the
beaver pelts to Bailly in the spring of
the year; he shipped them to Mackinac.
From there they traveled to Montreal
and eventually to Europe.

By 1830 Bailly's fur trading business
had nearly ended. Overtrapping had
nearly depleted the beaver population in
the area and the beaver felt hat had
gone out of style. In the early 1830's
Joseph Bailly opened a tavern
northwest of the homestead on the Fort
Dearborn to Detroit Road (present day
U.S. Hwy. 12) to supplement his
income. The fur trading era in
northwestern Indiana had come to an
end.

Photo courtesy Indiana Dunes National Lakeshore.

Chapter 15:

Fur Trader Joseph Bailly and the Homestead He Left Behind

It is a crisp fall day in woods just two miles south of the tip of Lake Michigan in the Indiana Dunes National Lakeshore. My wife and I had already explored the old farmhouse on the adjacent Chellberg Farm, established by Swedish immigrants, and were on our way down the trail southward to the one-time property of an early day fur trader named Joseph Bailly, the first white settler in northwest Indiana.

The Bailly homestead was a center of warm hospitality for travelers between Chicago and Detroit. Though pioneers in the wilderness, the family was well cultured and well educated. (Photo Indiana Dunes National Lakeshore)

We looked ahead toward a wooded hollow and saw puffs of white smoke arise from a small clearing. Its fragrant smell drifted our way. We seemed to see an Indian teepee, some outbuildings, a log cabin and a few people absorbing this nostalgic setting. Is that really a fur trader hanging out around the cabin door?

There was a peaceful quiet in the air, even though we were but a mile from the upper Midwest's foremost coast to coast highway. Have we really stepped back into time?

That's exactly what the National Park Service wants you to feel as you take in the annual fall festival at the Joseph Bailly Homestead, registered in 1962 as a National Landmark, and located in Porter County, half way between Gary and Michigan City.

So who was Joseph Bailly? Well, he was a French Canadian and devout Catholic who had worked the fur trade around Mackinac even as a teenager, then moved down to Lake Michigan's southern shores and the Kankakee River. He was cleared as an independent trapper to establish a fur trade with the Indians in that region. His fur trade peaked around 1800. John Jacob Astor established his far-reaching American Fur Company in 1808, but despite his clout his firm never could monopolize the trade. Independents still flourished.

At times the British had muddled the waters. Though the Revolutionary War had defeated them, they were slow to abandon their own lucrative fur trade in America and, in fact, did not even give up Detroit until 1792. Let's remember they even burned the U.S. Capitol as late as 1812! Records say that in 1813 Bailly himself was charged as pro British, though without substance.

The French had freely roamed the Great Lakes region but in 1801 Napoleon sold a major part of the Midwest to the Americans for a song. In 1822 Bailly obtained permission from the United States and the Indians to settle on high ground close to the Little Calumet River, along the Chicago to Detroit Road, also regarded as the old Great Sauk Trail.

Though living in such primitive setting, members of the Bailly family were hardly uneducated, rough-hewn creatures of the wilderness. Joseph was an outstanding lecturer in history and geography, equipped to educate curious Indians eager to hear about the white man's country. The four Bailly girls spoke the Indian, French and English languages fluently. For the benefit of Indians, the oldest translated the Latin mass for traveling priests. The daughters were also well-trained musicians.

Bailly furnishings in this wilderness setting included mahogany furniture, but also Indian-made articles, some crude, others beautiful. It included books, sterling silver, china dishes, a piano and other musical instruments.

The homestead was a center for hospitality. Joseph Bailly taught religion and accommodated traveling priests and used the family dining room to celebrate Mass, Indians and others invited. The homestead was the only Catholic mission between Detroit and Chicago. In the French Canadian era the government had required that a missionary be stationed at each French trading post. Bailly later built a church on the premises.

Though quiet and remote today, the Bailly homestead was an active way station of earlier times, with fur traders and Indians coming and going. And that's the kind of history that intrigues archaeologists, convinced there must be items buried somewhere there in the soil that could reveal the past.

So it should be no surprise that in 2012 a contingent of students from Notre Dame, spurred by an archaeology professor, undertook a dig on Bailly grounds to uncover--who knows what? With all the "traffic" there in the fur trade era, they reasoned, they should come up with some finds, and, after all, the history of this ground would go back not just a couple of hundred years, but even into prehistoric times.

This author has yet to learn if any of their archaeological dreams were realized.

Chapter 16:

From the Fighting Irish To the Hobart Brickies

The legends of yesteryear stretch from the turf of leprechauns to Yohan Petrovich

      Notre Dame football has long dominated the sports history of northwest Indiana. If you want to walk in the hallowed footsteps of names like Knute Rockne and all the other coaches and Heisman Trophy winners and stars of its glorious past, it means a visit to this campus and stadium.

      Though its football history goes back to 1887, the Irish lost its first game to Michigan and did not defeat them until 1909, after which Michigan refused to play Notre Dame for the next 33 years. Notre Dame was still somewhat small time until in 1913 Coach Jesse Harper scheduled games with Texas, Penn State and Army to gain national respect. Notre Dame stunned Army 35-13 at West Point. Player Knute Rockne, soon to become a legend, played end receiver and in this game he firmly established the forward pass. Previously receivers would come to a dead stop and simply wait for the ball. The forward pass changed football offense.

Knute Rockne became the Irish coach in 1918. In the next 13 years he would win 105 games, three national championships and the 1925 Rose Bowl. In those years he gave his famous locker room *Win One for the Gipper* speech , during half time at an Army game that looked like a sure loss. Notre Dame came from behind to upset Army and win the game 12-6.

Those who might escort you on a tour of Notre Dame's stadium today will take you by the memorial to Knute Rockne and tell you that he was to this stadium like Babe Ruth was to Yankee Stadium, "the house that Ruth built." From the national following Rockne generated in his time came the resources to build Notre Dame Stadium in 1930.. Rockne even designed the stadium, though he coached in it only one year before he was killed in a tragic plane crash.

Notre Dame football glory lives on to this day, though the sport was de-emphasized for atime to stress academics. The program resumed

Oscar Rabe Hanson,1925 Lithograph
Courtesy Calumet Regional Archives
Indiana University Northwest.

Notre Dame football coach Knute Rockne talks to fullback Joe Savoldi at the Chicago auto show just two months before his tragic death when his flight from Chicago to Los Angeles caught fire in mid air over Kansas. (Google Images)

in 1997 and its stadium was even enlarged from a capacity of 56,000 to more than 80,000.

Though far more obscure to the public at large than Notre Dame's stadium backdropped by the school's famous golden dome, there's another stadium in northwest Indiana known to the locals that should not go unmentioned. It requires that we drop down to the high school level, but be it known that ESPN has ranked it sixth among the top ten high school stadiums in the nation.

Yes, it's Hobart's Brickie Bowl, now pretty much abandoned but perhaps destined for some kind of renewal and it may even be designated as an historical landmark.

Its unique setting and history has been described this way by ESPN:

"Constructed in 1939 by the Works Progress Administration (WPA), it sits near the district's middle school in a downtown area with no true parking lot. Duck Creek runs under the aluminum bleachers on the visitors' side and circles the east end of the stadium. Train tracks run directly behind and above the visitors' seats. The trains often pass by during games, sounding their horns only when Hobart opponents are on offense.

"When the river flows the field is flooded with water and fish. The west side opens up to several homes sometimes filled with tailgating parties and bonfires. Hobart has been to 11 state finals and once completed a 71-game winning streak."
Add to this unique setting a football team called "the Brickies." The what? There's no other high school team in the nation with such a label. They were named for the local brickyards that existed in earlier days. Now let's meet their unusual mascot, Yohan Petrovich, whose name appeared on a study hall list for days in 1942, the figment of then student George Zupko's imagination as he drew sketches of him as if doodling. Yohan's impressive physique was developed, so goes the

legend, by building bricks from the years he spent in the brickyards of Hobart. The student cartoon

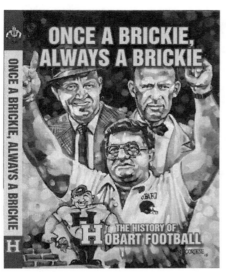

was eventually picked up as the school's trademark, and hefty plastic statues of Yohan Petrovich, with trowel of cement in one hand and a brick in the other, can be seen around this town.

Whether in South Bend or Hobart, you'll find yesteryear just around the corner.

Footnote: To order the book, Once a Brickie Always a Brickie, The History of Hobart Football, by Paul Condry, click on to hobartschoolhotwires.com or www.HobartBrickieFootball.com.

Buffalo on the Broken Wagon Bison Ranch.

Chapter 17:

We've a Herd of Buffalo Out Here in Our County!!

You've got to be kidding! This isn't your proverbial 'home on the range.'

A herd of buffalo roaming on the edge of town? Just because you may have never seen these guys doesn't mean they're not out there on the landscape west of Valparaiso. It's called the Broken Wagon Bison Ranch, co-owned by Bud Koeppen and his brother Wally. Though located in Porter County, their official address is Hobart.

The buffalo roam freely on 45 acres, but in the summer you can tour the herd on a wagon and roam among these American icons yourself, but just don't get off to pet them. That stare they'll give you is not ominous; they're just curious. Big John the bull weighs at least two thousand pounds, but he may be the friendliest of them all and he likes his picture taken.

So how did these two third generation farmers who once grew only corn and soybeans wind up with a herd of buffalo?

It all started, says Bud, when he got a Christmas card from the photographer who had taken his wedding picture decades ago. The man had acquired acreage near Rockville, built himself a log cabin and bought bison. That started a conversation and in 2003 the Koeppen brothers added a few bison of their own to their existing farm operations. The herd expanded. Recently at a convention in Denver the National Bison Association named Bud its Member of the Year.

Some 60-70 million bison once roamed the central plains of America, from the Rockies to the Mississippi and from Canada to Mexico. In the advance of the American frontier the history of the buffalo turned tragic. The slaughter was aided by the emergence of the transcontinental railroad. Millions of buffalo were shot simply for sport, or

The transcontinental railroad and the buffalo.
(Associated Press Photo Archives)

for their tongues and hides, or for profit, the rest of the animal left to rot. Destroy the buffalo, military authorities said, and it will force the Indians onto reservations. By the turn of the century only an estimated 325 buffalo remained in America and at that time it seemed sure they would become extinct had it not been for a handful of ranchers like famed Texas cattleman Charles Goodnight, who as far back as 1866 had organized the first cattle drive from Texas to Kansas and also invented the chuckwagon. His story later inspired the movie *Lonesome Dove.*

At the encouragement of his wife Goodnight had rescued a few orphan buffalo calves and established his own private little herd.

At the time I first met Bud Koeppen he had just returned from a visit to the historic Goodnight ranch near Amarillo, Texas. "Descendants of that early day herd," he says, "are still on the property.

Legendary South Dakota rancher Scotty Phillips established the nucleus of the herd that today populates Custer State Park. "He was so revered," says Koeppen, "that upon his death the Chicago and Northwestern Railroad ran special

The annual buffalo roundup at Custer State Park.
Historians attribute the rescue of the American
buffalo in part to a handful of western ranchers.

trains and paid free passage to his funeral. He was buried next to Bison pasture and it was said that as he was laid to rest hundreds of Bison came over the hill and lined the fence, paying their last respects."

Tycoon broadcaster Ted Turner owns some 50,000 head of today's estimated 400,000 buffalo population in North America, spread over more than fifteen ranches and two million acres.

The Broken Wagon Ranch runs around one hundred head of buffalo. At one time only about 325 bison still existed in the United States

After briefing ranch visitors Bud Koeppen invites them to look out over the buffalo in his pasture and multiply by three. "That's all there were," he says. "Ponder just how close we came to losing this animal forever."

This author remembers watching a thundering herd of buffalo suddenly tumbling to its demise over a high cliff. It was a western movie, the buffalo either off course or running from "the bad guys." I can't recall. Western movies may have romanticized the buffalo, but one wonders how Hollywood could have assembled the numbers for a stampede, given the tragic destruction of the buffalo by the time Hollywood got on the scene. Zane Grey's novel, *The Thundering Herd,* prompted a 1933 Western film starring Randolph Scott. When buffalo stampede, the ground shakes and the owners of the Broken Wagon Bison Ranch will tell you that their herd too shakes the earth when they all run together, sometimes at 35-50 miles an hour.

To everyone's delight the buffalo has made a comeback, its population now one half million. Only 20,000 run free, though now some of these can be found only 95 miles west of Chicago. The Nachusa Grasslands, a 3,500 acre prairie restoration project near Franklin, Illinois, accommodates a small herd.

In the restoration of the prairies that once covered mid America, planted herds of bison are considered the centerpieces, but it will take time for the prairie's one-time ecology to restore itself. This effort may also bring back the prairie dog.

While bison farms of limited acreage cannot let bison roam totally free and without fencing, owners of the Broken Wagon operation say their biggest reward is seeing their bison "frolicking and playing in the snow as happy as can be." They do require six-foot fences. Buffalo seldom get sick and they need no shelter in the winter. They have great immune systems. Bison live about fifteen years in the wilds but up to 40 years in captivity.

Are buffalo and bison the same? Authorities say yes. It's a matter of terminology, though the word "buffalo" seems to have an older origin. Its usage in America dates to 1675 and originated with the French fur trappers. The word "bison" derives from a Greek word and was first recorded in 1774. Bison are not related to the Water Buffalo of Asia.

The Indians wasted no part of the buffalo, turning the animal into more than one hundred uses. From their bones they made tools and weapons. From their hides they made blankets, clothing and teepees.

When you tour the Broken Wagon Bison Ranch you'll want to browse in their gift shop. There you'll find "all things buffalo." Rugs. Soaps. Purses. Pillows. Gloves. Toys. Books. Jerky. Other leather products.

Then there's the buffalo meat itself. When not long ago I spent a day at the fur trader's Voyageurs Rendezvous at Hobart's Maple Lake, I opted for a bison sandwich over a hot dog. The meat had come from the Broken Wagon Bison

Ranch, after first going through a government-approved processing firm. The meat is sweet tasting, healthy. Nor have buffalo been raised on hormones. The farm will encourage you to try it, or fulfill your re-order. Some folk are regular customers. And the owners are a friendly people. You'll feel at home on the range.

Despite the tragic history of the buffalo in the earlier years of our nation, the animal is still an American icon. So go ahead, let yourself get buffaloed, defined by *Webster's Dictionary* as not simply baffled, but overawed. Let your tour of this Porter County bison ranch that you probably didn't even know existed take you back in time.

Yesteryear is just around the corner.

For a video interview at the Broken Wagon Bison Ranch by reporter Jesse Harper click on to You Tube (6:42 min.)

Pour it on your pancakes right off a hot griddle.
(Photo courtesy Parke County Covered Bridge Festival.)

Chapter 18:
Maple Syrup Time
In Northwest Indiana

There have been several ways to make it.
It depends on what era you want to re-live.

Maple syrup. Did it not once come in a tin log cabin? They called it "Log Cabin Syrup." The metal cabin fascinated me as a kid. Then it became too expensive for General Foods to market this sugary product in such a container

Cold March weather froze this maple syrup on the Chellberg farm in Dunes National Lakeshore. (Photo courtesy the National Park Service.)

and the cans were also hard to stack on grocery shelves. You can still buy the container on e-bay, including a 1987 edition celebrating the 100th anniversary of this Log Cabin product first introduced in 1887.The Potawatomi Indians, however, and other tribes across eastern America, were producing maple syrup long before General Foods. And several historical sites close by can show you how they did it.

They'll tell you they would take the sap from maple trees, pour it into hollowed out logs or clay pots and then place it on an open fire, where it would gradually thicken. It was a product that not only satisfied the tribe's own appetite but it could also be used for trade.

When Europeans introduced metal to the New World the sap was often cooked in large cast iron kettles. When Swedish settlers carved out their farms in the Porter County dunes, they boiled the sap down in large flat pans, so the water in the sap could evaporate more quickly.

Every year on the first two weekends of March at the Chellberg Farm on Mineral Springs Road in the Dunes National Lakeshore you can walk its property and be briefed on how the early pioneers did it. In this primitive setting you can take a self-guided tour or let park rangers along the trail explain the process. Kids can even drill a tap hole and shoulder an old fashioned yolk like those that helped pioneers carry the sap buckets

Wood smoke scents the landscape, the Lion's Club serves up sausage and pancakes and guides lead you to the Chellberg Swedish homestead and its parlor, where they'll challenge you in a taste test to compare their "homegrown" maple syrup to that from a grocery store. One volunteer has been known simply to call the latter an "imposter" and to tell the people "It's the difference between Folgers and Starbucks."

Chellberg's Maple Syrup Time has been an annual event now for nearly 40 years. March's weather in northwest Indiana can be fickle. It can range anywhere from snow to weather for "a light jacket." The event can be a great learning experience for families with children, though at least one solely adult group from Lansing makes the outing every year.

More than ten miles to the south of the National Lakeshore you can find another great venue for the maple sugar experience. It is the Deep River County Park on Hobart's southeast perimeter. Though just across Hwy 30 from northwest Indiana's largest water park, your short hike into these woods will feel like a trek into the frontier past, given the rippling sounds of the creek meandering through the dense woods and an adjacent old grist mill with its water wheel. In real history, this was indeed the historic Sauk Trail of Native Americans and early pioneers.

Here too Maple Syrup Time waits for the weather that is below freezing at night and about 40 degrees in the day.

Deep River offers the attraction of its rustic sugar shack, set in a forested glade and where a wood-fired burner evaporates the sap's water content. Maple Syrup Time here has now added the Voyagers, dressed in the authentic clothing of frontier traders. They will tell you how valuable maple syrup was for the diet of early America's Indians, who boiled it with their vegetables and meat. Every half hour offers an educational video, and at the gift shop you can buy maple sugar and maple candy. Add maple iced donuts, maple tea, coffee, hot chocolate and the corn meal you can watch them grind on the spot. Or you can watch the skills of a weaver, or study a whittler carving his creation or play checkers in front of the stove. The entire experience, apart from the products you might buy, is free.

Waukarusa just southeast of South Bend touts its own annual Maple Syrup Festival in late April, a major event for that town, though not held in a time of sap flow. The event includes a parade, antique show, vendors and entertainment. Its website will intrigue you with an old Iriquois Indian legend on the "discovery" of maple syrup.

It seems Chief "Worksis", out hunting one day, yanked a tomahawk from a tree where he had left it the evening before. The weather had turned warm that night and sap dripped into a pot that happened to stand close to the base of the tree. The chief's wife picked up the pot to save her another trip for water to boil. Once heated, she tasted it sweet contents, rather liked it so she used it for cooking water. When the chief returned home to his tepee he savored the smell of what now had become maple syrup. And that's how it all started.

Critics point out, though, that until the time of Columbus the Indians were a stone-age people, with no skills to make a metal pot. Instead, they heated rocks on an open fire, used sticks to transfer them into wooden bowls of sap and replaced each rock with a freshly heated one once the prior one cooled.

The Iriquois legend is warm and fuzzy, but I'll take the story of the rocks.

A young cowboy looks after his horse at early July's LaPorte County Fair, oldest fair in Indiana. Porter and Lake County fairs follow.
(What's New LaPorte? Bob Wellsinski/Mike Kellem)

Chapter 19:

Enjoy Americana at Its Best at Your Local County Fair

Lake, Porter and LaPorte counties all mix family fun with past heritage.

Fairs are the stuff of a nation's heritage, its past, its future. They've also been settings for classic movies cast in the turn of the century culture. Who of today's older generations have not seen "Meet Me in St. Louis," starring Judy Garland and Margaret O'Brien, with a story line connected to that city's 1903 World's Fair. Or "State Fair," its setting in Iowa, with a lovable pig named "Blue Boy" as one of its top stars. Two other vintage movies have story lines associated with the Iowa State Fair.

County fairs are smaller and more local, of course, but the format is similar. Though one can trace the roots of the fair to Europe, American fairs dating back to 1810 were established by agriculture to educate farmers. Manufacturers also saw the potential and signed on to show off their latest plows, planters and reapers.

The LaPorte County Fair, oldest in Indiana, emerged in 1845. Building on its agricultural focus, it eventually added such domestic realms as canning, sewing, crafts, fine arts and painting. After the turn of the century came a vigorous 4-H movement, which expanded rapidly and remains strong today in the fair's mix.

The LaPorte fair added its highly popular Pioneer Land in 1997, an 1800s village ideal for the education of school children. It includes a general store, blacksmith shop, quilters cabin, antique barn, artisan barn, garden and a Farm Bureau log cabin. The LaPorte County Fair usually runs for seven days in early July.

If you're a county fair buff you can follow up with the Porter County fair the second half of July, which normally runs ten days. A scan of a typical daily schedule reveals a broad list of events that would reflect the feel of yesteryear. How about an antique machinery exhibit, a 4-H draft horse show, a Country Showdown and the Good Time Cloggers? Throw in a Country Barnyard exhibit, pig races and a popular rodeo.

Most urban children today never hear the crow of a rooster, but unfortunately in 2015 Indiana had to prohibit the showing of poultry at its fairs statewide because of the bird flu scare.

The Lake County Fair in Crown Point follows in August. It too is ten days and draws the largest total attendance simply because it's in an area of greater population.

It too has had some eye-catching features, like its Demo Derby, Western Horse Show, draft horses, frog jump contest and free fireworks. The Farm Bureau throws in a "Farm to Fork" quick and easy meals demonstration, kids get a camel ride, Indiana woodworkers demonstrate their skills and this crowd too often races pigs. Music ranges from 60s garage rock to bluegrass,

He wants to be sure the carnival midway and big name entertainers don't hog the show.

country and gospel. The precise mix of events can change from year to year.

At all of these county fairs there are always livestock events unfolding on the fairgrounds simultaneously. Even cattle and pigs and cows and sheep and goats don't like to be left behind. Farm kids hang out day to day with both their animals and their peers. These will become some of their best memories later in life. Throw in a carnival, of course, and on-stage entertainment.

At a fair children can see first hand why milk in a carton comes from more than a grocery store.
(What's New LaPorte? Bob Wellsinski/Mike Kellem)

Swedish immigrants approach Ellis Island.
(Associated Press Archives, circa 1900)

Chapter 20:

A Swedish American Story Unfolds in the Indiana Dunes

It was at a Scanadinvian Midsummer Celebration at the Chellberg Farm

The event is a centuries-old tradition in Sweden, held during the summer solstice, translated as the first day of summer.

Children from Nordikids in Munster, led by director Lennea Sinweiski, decorated a Maypole with flowers, danced around it and sang Swedish songs for visitors, one song rehearsing immigrant longing for friends and family left back in the old country.

Marilyn Arvidson, a volunteer with the event at Indiana Dunes, teared up as the kids sang "Halsa Dem Darhemma" in Swedish, not an easy language to learn. She remembered her own father's struggles to build a life in America.

If you listen to Celtic music, and particularly its lyrics, you'll hear songs reflecting this same kind of struggle as immigrants left their beloved Ireland, perhaps during the potato famine, to carve out their living on a new continent.

On this day at Chellberg Farm (the name spelled Kjellberg in Swedish) those attending joined in traditional Swedish games like dropping clothes pins into glass milk bottles, tossing rings and throwing corn cobs.

My wife and I are not Swedish, but we worshipped for years in two Swedish-rooted churches and cherished such friends as the late Stig and Olna Momquist, former owners of the Scandanavian Boutique across the Illinois border in Homewood. A mover and shaker then in Chicago's Swedish American Society, still with her old country accent and fluent in Swedish, she would always be sure she greeted the King of Sweden when he came to Chicago.

The Chellberg Farm lets you see and feel the setting of this family on its dunes property, occupied by three generations until it was sold in 1972 to the National Park Service.

The arrival of the railroad and a good job market attracted Anders Chellberg to this site after his arrival from Sweden in the 1850s. He lost no time recruiting other immigrants as well. A significant cluster of Swedish folk settled in Northwest Indiana when they were displaced by The Great Chicago Fire of 1871. Unfortunately, the original Chellberg farmhouse itself was later

The Chellberg house, built of brick after their original wooden structure burned. Some Swedes displaced by the Chicago fire moved to Indiana. (Photo Indiana Dunes National Lakeshore.)

destroyed by fire. The family re-built with brick, taking advantage of the clay in Porter County.

Your tour of this farm includes its 1885 Victorian style brick farmhouse, the original barn, a corn crib, a chicken coop, a chapel and, at your discretion, a more distant cemetery.

The Chellberg story parallels my own farm background in the West. The Chellberg family took legal title to its property in 1869, the same year my own great grandmother had rumbled West by wagon train and settled in the back country of California's San Andreas Fault. The

Chellbergs cleared their land for farming at a rate of about ten acres a year. My ancestors found enough open land to avoid that process. The Chellberg farm included wheat, horses, sheep, swine and poultry.

During the Civil War Indiana, Illinois and Wisconsin produced the most wheat, but the encroachment of corn and rising real estate values kept pushing wheat on beyond the Mississippi. Yet by 1872 California produced more wheat than Kansas! Wheat suddenly exploded out West with arrival of the transcontinental railroad. The Chellberg farm could prosper too after the railroad arrived.

No tractors existed then, though by 1920 my maternal grandmother was working the telephone switchboard at Stockton, California's Holt Manufacturing, Benjamin Holt the inventor of the Caterpillar. Salesmen pushing the tractor faced a major problem. Farmers didn't know what to do with their horses. It was a sentimental thing and probably so also for the Chellbergs.

The Chellbergs raised sheep. They didn't have to go far to buy them. The Far West? In 1852 California rancher clans Flint and Bixby, with nearly 50 cowhands and four cowgirls, rode horseback to the Midwest, bought ten thousand sheep in Ohio and Missouri and drove them to California. That historic transcontinental sheep

A picnic crowd gathers at the Chellberg barn.
(Photo Indiana Dunes National Lakeshore)

drive took a year and a half. Only a thousand sheep made it, but once there the lucky ones thrived under the care of Basque sheepherders. By the 1880s California had 8 million sheep

The Chellberg barn is the original structure but most barns of that vintage no longer stand. Read on for "The Rise and Fall of the Counryside Barn" (chapter 22). The Chellbergs added on to their original farmhouse. With most old farm homes still standing today you can detect the additions, perhaps dictated by a good crop year, suggesting prosperity, or an ever growing family.

By the 1950s, with third generation

Chellbergs in charge, the farm could no longer sustain them. Carl took a job at a machine shop in Chesterton and his wife cooked at a nearby

restaurant. The farm became secondary. And so it is with many farmers today unless they own or lease a lot of acreage.

There often comes a time when the family farm of "yesteryear" has to become only memories. It was so in my family. It was so with the Chellbergs.

Beth Shubair (nee Chellbereg), pictured above, a great granddaughter of Anders and Johanna Chellberg, often volunteered at the Indiana Dunes farm and enjoyed telling stories of her Swedish ancestors. A 1959 graduate of Chesterton High School, she worked for *Fortune* magazine but put her career on hold to raise her family. She died in 2012.

Taltree Garden Railroad, Valparaiso

Chapter 21:

The Taltree Garden Railroad and the Illiana Garden Railway

Both in Valparaiso, their landscapes show remarkable detail. They'll take you back into America's yesteryear.

Years ago my next door neighbor one day started hauling in big rocks and boulders just across our fence line. He told me he was going to build a garden railroad. He opened a hobbyist magazine and handed it to me across the fence to show me a sample photo from the article he was using to help him build his dream project. Incredibly its author, with whom my neighbor had been consulting by phone two thousand miles across the country to San Luis Obispo, California, had once been an old friend and Cal Poly classmate of mine. We had even once sung together on that campus in a barber shop group called "The Majors and Minors." It put the two of us back in contact after more than 30 years.

I was excited about our neighbor's plans. It would be a great attraction to point out as we escorted occasional guests through our own well landscaped property. Kids would love it.

In time it began to take shape: a rock mountain, a track, a trestle, a few plants. Then my neighbor, himself a railroad executive, was suddenly transferred to Pueblo, Colorado. He sold the house to new owners who didn't know what to do with the pile of rocks in their backyard. They just left them there, engulfed in weeds. I was disappointed..

You won't be disappointed by the two garden railroads in Valparaiso, Porter County, one at Taltree arboretum and the other a short distance off the Indiana tollway. While only a few miles apart, each is distinctive. Both are garden gauge

(G-gauge) and both are, as you might expect, outdoors.

Let's first visit Taltree, with its woodland trails, pond, small prairie and concert venue. It's a great place for a quiet walk, but if it's your first time its miniature railroad is a must. Its owners call it the largest public railway garden in the Midwest. Those who brief you will make what you see come alive in the context of America's railroad history.

Its architects have blended a wide range of landscapes into its sprawling layout. Trains run through canyons, mountains, prairies, shuttling farm products, steel, lumber and more. One family on their way to the National Garden Railway convention held that year in Akron, Ohio, suggested later in retrospect that visitors here should bring their binoculars. The father took more than one hundred photos, including close-ups, only to discover when they looked at them back home details they had missed: like a woman carrying a child from a bakery and two ladies having tea on a roof.

A vintage depot alongside the outdoor exhibit houses railroad memorabilia, a gift shop and a setting for children's birthday parties. Located at 450 W. 100 North, the exhibit is open April to October.

The Illiana Railroad on North State Rd. 2 shows off its "Bull Moose Line, whose right-of-ways are backdropped by mountains, a three tiered waterfall and a mill pond. Its outdoor

Illiana Railway's Bull Moose Line, Valparaiso (Courtesy Senior Life magazine)

diorama takes you through the rural farming township of Franville, by a gold mine and into an industrial switchyard complete with a roundhouse and engine turntable. Its newly installed command system can handle six trains at a time.

Meanwhile, a vintage streetcar winds around Franville from the train station to a ballpark. Youngsters can watch "Thomas the Train" run on its own special track above the township and across the upper waterfall.

If you want to learn the lingo of the railroad, even among serious model railroad enthusiasts, Al Gengler, writing for the Illiana Garden Railway Society (IRGS), offers his A-Z

"Moose Tracks Glossary" which you can access on the IRGS website. Here are just a few examples from the latter part of the alphabet:

> **Throttle jerker:** railroad engineer.
> **Throw out the anchor**: done for the day.
> **Tie 'em down:** set handbrakes.
> **Top dresser drawer:** Upper bunk in
> caboose.
> **Uncle Sam:** Railway Post Office clerk.
> **Underground Hog:** Chief engineer.
> **Unload:** Get off train hurriedly.
> **Vaseline:** Oil.

Membership in the non-profit Illiana Garden Railway Society, which formed in 2003, is open to model railroad enthusiasts in Indiana, Michigan and Illinois. It is working with another non-profit organization to build, possibly, the largest garden railroad in the country. The Illiana Garden Railway is open to the public each Saturday, May-September, weather permitting.

The history of America and that of its railroads are intertwined. Look for a railroad exhibit and you'll be sure to walk back into yesteryear.

Each year thousands of old barns across America are either torn down or they fall down. Billboard barns urging one to chew Mail Pouch tobacco have all but vanished, although you can find a collection of them on the web. Barn advertising was most popular from 1900-1940, but it was estimated that 20,000 still remained as late as 1960. One prolific artist claimed to have painted some 20,000 barns in his lifetime, taking an average of six hours for each. He always started with the letter "e".

Chapter 22:

The Rise and Fall of Old Country Barns

Every old barn has its life, its history, its story. Sometimes it's a shaky one.

Any drive out into the countryside will favor you with an assortment of old barns. They can be fascinating. Some look well kept, maybe painted red, still functional, an asset on the property, sometimes much better looking than the owner's adjacent farm house.

Others seem a disgrace, but don't be too judgmental. The owners may be preserving their memories and family heritage, at least until their aging parents leave the earth. The barn may still protect some old farm equipment.

The barn may be artistic. People paint them. Photograph them.

Some owners turn them into great commercial value, like Hobart's highly successful County Line Apple Orchard, now a sprawling complex gracing a pleasant 37-acre landscape at

County Line Orchard's apple grove and sprawling "country shopping mall" takes you into the past. (Photo courtesy Luke Oil.)

the edge of town. It' s a great place to step back into yesteryear.

OK, so the main barn, built in this decade, is not a vintage structure, but it is an impressive expansion to the original complex. It's doubtful any of the early Lake or Porter County settlers ever saw a barn this big. Nor does it have any live cows--only its little Moo train that takes the kids through a dense grove of old oak trees.

The barn's interior resembles a rustic shopping mall, with about anything you can imagine that fit's the country theme. One soon picks up the aroma of apple cider and fresh

This barn in rural Portage still carries a vintage Mail Pouch tobacco graphic along with a happy face. Do you know just where it is? (Photo credit Wikivoyage. Public domain).

donuts. Roam the balconies for all kinds of country craft and wall décor.

At the heart of this operation, though, is its apple orchard, drawing thousands who show up in the fall to pick their own apples, walk its fall corn maze and buy a pumpkin. For city school kids who pour in each day in yellow buses, many from Chicago, it's a day in the country.

It's also a venue for special events and weddings. The owners, Luke Oil, even incorporated an old silo into the huge new addition, where the bride of the wedding can emerge on its lofty balcony to wave at the crowd below. That's offering newlyweds extra milage on their rental of a barn. I said milage, not silage. I like the architect's creative blend of a silo. My wife and I once attended the dedication of a new rural church created from a renovated barn. The pastor had taken the silo for his office.

I wonder how many old barns disappear from the American landscape each year. They're either torn down or they fall down. And it's getting harder than ever to find one that still says, "Chew Mail Pouch Tobacco."

In weddings held at the County Line Orchard's rambling barn in Hobart an attached silo allows the bride to emerge through a door onto its high side balcony and wave to the crowd below. That gets the bride extra milage on her wedding package. I said milage, not silage.

Since this author grew up on a grain ranch in the Far West, I'll shift from the Hoosier landscape for a moment to recount the rise and fall of our family barn that, incredibly, directly straddled California's San Andreas Fault! Hang on to the end. The story is a shaky one.

The San Andreas Fault tracked directly under the middle of our family barn, built in the early days. In 1922 a major earthquake struck in early morning darkness. An old hobo had chosen that night to bed down there. He fled the scene and disappeared, not bothering to shut the barn door.

Over decades the barn further deteriorated, its roof line ever more swayback like the back of the one remaining old horse on our property, the family's last vestige of the horse and plow. But the barn's greatest fame still lay ahead.

In the early 60s seismologists from the California Institute of Technology in Pasadena took special note of this obscure and remote little valley in the back country and its tiny hamlet of Parkfield, population 37. They detected a regular pattern of earthquakes here so they planted seismic instruments in our barn and assigned my stepfather to monitor them, sending monthly reports to Cal Tech. It was easier to pay an on site wheat and barley rancher than to plant a resident seismologist in the valley, although they eventually did so. The instruments picked up earthquakes as far away as Turkey.

The fault tracked between our house and our chicken pens, two great continental plates scraping one another, the fault at this point camouflaged by dirt until opened by a fresh earthquake. Our chickens clucked away on the American Plate, which seismologists told us extended all the way to Iceland. Our farm house sat on the Pacific Plate, which extended to Japan. That meant we gathered our eggs on one plate and ate them on the other! Forgive me.

After a major 1966 earthquake seismologists theorized that earthquakes in this valley had established an historical pattern. This might be the perfect site, they reasoned, to predict an earthquake. It would establish a first in the scientific world. With excitement they identified

1988 as the big year and began to riddle the valley with what became the largest cluster of seismic instruments on earth. Our little hamlet six miles to the north began to get national press.

A visionary cattle rancher built a log café in town and labeled it "The earthquake capitol of the world." Its motto: "Be here when it happens." It became the only town in America that invited you to an earthquake. Its menu, serving delicious tri-tip barbecues, included a SeismicBurger, a tossed salad and a San Andreas Shake. Appetizers were foreshocks, desserts aftershocks. In "the middle of nowhere" the café prospered.

The town threw its first Earthquake Dance and made the front page of *USA Today*. As the 1988 year of "The Big One" approached, media of every kind began to rush in: radio, TV, newspapers, magazines. Some journalists landed by helicopter. The BBC showed up from London with a full television team. *National Geographic* captured children in the town's one-room school with hands overhead, ducked under their desks in an "earthquake alert." The fault line through a hillside our family once farmed got half page coverage in the *New York Times*.

The media hung around for a big story. They waited. And waited. Nothing happened. They finally went home. The much hyped "Big One" did not hit until 2004, sixteen years late.

Earthquakes finally collapsed the family barn that straddled the San Andreas Fault. Midwest barns destroyed by natural disaster would likely be hit by a tornado (Photo by the author)

Seismologists were highly embarrassed. Some speculated that a 1983 earthquake on the fault line 30 miles north near the oil town of Coalinga may have relieved enough energy to throw off the calculation. Or was the initial premise faulty? Seismologists have since discarded the word "prediction," adopted the term "probability" and decided they may never be able to "predict" earthquakes.

The old barn? Well, it finally, collapsed, pulled apart by the strains of the San Andreas Fault. Its roof had lost half its shakes but the old barn couldn't shake the real shake. It would have never won an architectural award, but it had served with distinction, hosting seismologists from as far as Japan, Europe and the Middle East. It had seen them come and go. For two decades it had sheltered the best of seismic technology.

It finally tired of living on the edge, but today this old barn is remembered by seismologists around the world.

A barn here in the Midwest would far more likely be hit by a tornado than an earthquake, though in 1803 the Midwest reeled to a great earthquake on Missouri's New Madrid Fault that changed the course of the Mississippi River and rang church bells as far as Boston.

Another such big one in the Midwest might be overdue, but let's hope that's not an event of yesteryear that's still around the corner.

Courtesy of Lake County Parks

Chapter 23:

Paddle into the Past by Kayak or Canoe

In the quiet streams and bayous on your own doorstep you can "drift" with LaSalle and the Potawatomis.

The tweets and rumbles of a fife and drum corps drift into the woods from a clearing that borders the waters of Hobart's Big Maple Lake. It appears to be a major encampment of sorts, with several canoes tied up along the shore line. You seem to have stepped back into the 18th century and a gathering of folk in most unusual dress trading furs on the frontier.

You've got it. It's the annual Voyageurs Rendezvous, normally held each May in Jasper County at Hebron on the Kankakee River's Grand Marsh, but this year bridge work at that site has shifted the event 20 miles to the north. One hundred costumed re-enactors, dressed as French Canadian Voyageurs, British and French militia, civilians and settlers joined by Native Americans stage the impressive gathering. The Lake County Park Department has arranged it all.

At opening ceremony the militias and civilians meet at the flagpole. One of the re-enactors raises a wampum belt as a gesture of welcome. The French, British and American flags are raised, each flag authentic to that time. A fife and drum corps plays the song of each nation. We didn't have *The Star Spangled Banner* then, so the musicians play the accepted tune *Chester*.

The real excitement begins when an hour later the voyageurs paddle around the bend from adjacent waters, their canoes stocked with goods they're ready to trade. The men immediately exchange gifts. Then the trade turns to the women for much of the day. The voyageurs specialize in textiles, the natives in furs.

These men in authentic vintage attire pull their canoe through shallow waters as they replicate the adventures of the fur trader of yesteryear. (Photo ActiveHistory.ca)

Beaver pelts are the most desired. The market in Europe for beaver hats is booming-- a symbol of the new frontier across the ocean. The trade is international. The fur from each kind of animal has its own market potential. Fine hair from an animal could be turned into paint brushes and even tooth brushes.

The two-day re-enactment throws in other events: canoe "bobber races," storytelling, and

At an encampment on the Grand Kankakee Marsh children learn how to weave a sash. Finds they make on a scavenger hunt can be traded for sea shells, which become money they can use at a children's trading post to buy other items. (Photo courtesy of Lake County Parks)

even a tomahawk throw for the older children. It's a great chance for the whole family to learn frontier history as everyone steps back into the past. "We're teaching history that the children aren't learning in school," quotes one enactor in the *Post Tribune*. Storyteller Malachi Spencer and her daughters model dresses of that time and then tell the children, "The more petticoats you had the wealthier you were. And there were no stores to shop at. You had to make your own clothes."

All enjoy hot food and cold Sarsaparilla. Yes, there are hamburgers, hot dogs and fries, but the menu also tries to be vintage. I opted for a buffalo burger and a bowl of wild rice cranberry soup.

One needs to remember that rivers were "the highways of yesteryear." There were no roads. Indian trails were primitive. In today's less primitive land you can still paddle the Deep River for up to 20 miles into Lake Michigan itself. It's muddy, it moves slow (about one mile per hour) and you'll pass a few scattered homes, mowed lawns and some pasture. A series of log jams may hamper your navigation, so you'll have to pick up your canoe and walk the bank, but that's all a part of the experience. The water level may be too low at times if there has been a shortage of rain. Spring is often the best time for such an adventure.

Your wilderness experience can start at Deep River County Park off Ainsworth Rd. It's a 6 mile canoe trip to the Arizona St. bridge north of 61st Avenue and from there another 11 miles through the bayous of Lake George and Hobart to your ultimate destination. Lake County Park authorities can supply all the details.

The land of Indiana's far north in frontier days, much of it swampy, was a hunters' paradise: abundant elk, deer; Robert de LaSalle's expedition even captured buffaloes in local marshes. Fur-bearing animals abounded: beaver, otter, mink. Add the raccoons and muskrats. Also fowl: wild turkeys, ducks, geese, prairie chickens, partridges, quail and wild pigeons that could nearly darken the sky..

While busy paddling, lets continue to drift back into history. We'll first travel downstream under the French flag. Explorer La Salle and his expedition rowed in from Michigan on the way to St. Louis in 1682, and though they didn't follow Deep River, they paddled the Kankakee River not far away. What is today Indiana and all land west to the Mississippi would remain under the French flag for nearly one hundred years until the Treaty of Paris in 1783, which ended the French and Indian War.

Now enter the British fur traders. They came in from the north, headquartered on Mackinaw Island. In 1774 the British Parliament passed the Quebec Act and extended their jurisdiction to the Mississippi and Ohio Rivers, where now you'll more likely see the British flag.

Spain's intrusion was only a blink. In 1781 a small band of Spanish soldiers from Fort St. Louis sneaked in from across the Mississippi and

The Potawatomi Indians began to relocate west of the Mississippi in the early 1800s after a treaty with the U.S. Government, but some chiefs were granted small parcels of land and allowed to stay. Lake George and what is now Hobart was divided among four Indian chiefs. (Photo source LiveBinders.com)

took the fort at St. Joseph in what is now Michigan. They held it for just one day, then retreated, never to return.

Paddle another mile into the year 1800. Indiana had just become a territory and the American Revolution had booted out the British, though the Redcoats came back to burn the U.S. Capitol in 1812. Guarding their fur trapping claims, they dragged their feet leaving Detroit. Nonetheless, look now for the American flag.

The Potawatomis? They were still around, but in 1835 they met with United States Commissioners in Chicago to negotiate a treaty, Tribal warriors gave up five million acres of land in Indiana, Michigan and Illinois to move west of

South Bend Tribune Graphic / Gregg Bender

Prior to 1852 the Grand Kankakee Marsh and its watershed was the largest wetlands region in North America, even bigger than the Florida Everglades. For native Americans it was also one of the richest hunting grounds on the continent.

the Mississippi. Some chiefs were given grants that allowed them to stay. This included four chiefs for whom authorities divided up Hobart.

OK, paddle now on downriver (running north) into what is today Lake George. Oops, it's not a lake but still a river. George Earle, a builder from England doing projects in Philadelphia, has not yet quite arrived to see the lake's potential and to dam it up for his sawmill and gristmill, the latter destroyed by fire in 1953. George Earle bought his land from the Potawatomis as they were slowly moving on West and campaigned to make the settlement and stagecoach stop of Liverpool the Lake County seat. That failed. It went to Crown Point.

Earle then shifted his vision five miles to the east, built his dam and mills, laid out the plats of a new town and named it Hobart.

Early settlers began to show up from the East, among them the Mundell family, a name still well known around Hobart. My wife attended Mundell Elementary School. The Hobart Historical Society, just across the street from the Maria Reiner Senior Citizens Center, exhibits the rope bed the Mundells brought with them by covered wagon.

So now you've paddled six miles to George Earle's dam, site of the town's now much touted Lake George Dam Duck Race. It's time to tie up your canoe and grab a bite at one of the town's Main Street restaurants, or open your sack lunch at the town's riverside Festival Park.

There's another way to maneuver the waters of Lake George. Try the kayak. One can be rented at Diver's Supply on Hobart's Main Street. The kayaks are the wide kind hard to tip over. It's a relatively new Lake George attraction that is sure to catch on with more folk.

If you simply want to go fishing, you can rent your boat at Lake George Bait and Tackle at the south end of the Wisconsin St. bridge. They also rent peddle boats, electric and non-electric.

Now if you don't want to paddle through the woodlands, you can peddle through them. Hobart has just closed the final gap in the Oak Savannah Trail, and that now allows you to bike all the way from Valparaiso to the Oak Ridge Prairie Park near Griffith. The trail takes its name from its unique ecosystem, a transitional zone between forest and prairie. From easy access in Hobart the trail west quickly takes you to the edges of Lake George, with its permanent population of geese, ducks and ring-billed gulls. A long footbridge takes you over the neck between the lake's two main bodies, where you'll look down on a broad field of lily pads rimming the main stream. If your timing is right you may be able to wave down at a kayaker making his way through the bayous.

Northwest Indiana may not be quite as wild as it was in the days of explorer LaSalle, the fur traders, the Potawatomis and George Earle, but there's still a lot of the wilderness feel left, especially if you want to paddle its waters or peddle its trails into yesteryear.

The painting "Paddle the Dunes," by artist Barbara Spies Labus, was released as a new South Shore poster to celebrate the Northwest Indiana Paddling Association and the Lake Michigan Water Trail, the largest loop water trail in the world.

Acknowledgments

- Albanese Candy, Hobart
- Associated Press Archives
- Bailly Homestead, Chesterton
- Broken Wagon Buffalo Ranch, Hobart, Budd and Wally Koeppen
- Buckley Homestead, Lowell
- Calumet Regional Archives, Steve McShane
- Chellberg Farm, Chesterton2
- County Line Orchard, Hobart, Ryan Richardson
- Dillinger Museum, Crown Point
- Duneland Tourism, Chesterton
- Flood, David, Country Barn Publishing
- Fulton, Robert, City of Hobart
- History Museum, South Bend, Brandon Anderson
- Hobart Chamber of Commerce, Lisa Winstead
- Hobart Historical Society, Rita McBride, Paula Isolampi
- Illiana Garden Railway
- Indiana Dunes National Lakeshore
- Kiwanis, Hobart: Evelyn Campbell, Gary Nagy
- Labus, Barbara Spies, artist

- Lake County Fair
- Lake County Parks, Chris Landgrave
- Library of Congress
- Lincoln's Theatre Carriage Museum
- Maria Reiner Center, Hobart, Pam Broadaway
- Markovitz, Mitch, artist
- Northwest Indiana Paddling Association, Dan Plath
- Notre Dame University, South Bend
- Ogden Dunes Historical Society, Ken Martin, Dick Meister
- Old Lighthouse Museum, Michigan City, Jim Restock
- Portage Historical Museum,
- Porter County Fair
- Studebaker Museum, South Bend, Andrew Beckman
- Talltree Nature Center, Valparaiso
- U.S. National Archives
- Valparaiso Opera House
- What's New LaPorte? Bob Wellsinski and Mike Kellems

Appendix:
Local Historical Museums

Local museums like those listed below can teach you much about the history, lifestyle and culture of days gone by. It's a great place to take children. Phone ahead or check their websites first, however, to learn what days they're open and if there's an upcoming special event.. All have limited hours and some are not open in the winter. Specifics listed are subject to change. You can also call the South Shore Convention and Visitors Authority or South Shore CVA at (219) 980-1617.

Buckley Homestead Living History Farm 3606 Bleshaw Road, Lowell, Indiana 48356 (Lake). Turn-of-the-century farming is preserved in every detail in this 1800's setting. Watch farm horses plow the fields, pet the barn animals, one-room schoolhouse or rustic cabin. In authentic costumes, the staff will show you around and recount for you pioneer days on the farm. Open May-Oct weekends 9AM-5PM, and weekends by reservations.

Joseph Hess Schoolhouse 7205 Kennedy Ave., Hammond, Indiana 46323 (Lake). Go back in time to 1869 in this little red schoolhouse, containing the original school bell, desks with inkwells, pot belly stove, books and 36-star flag. Open Apr-Oct., Sun 1-5PM, or by appointment.

LaPorte County Historical Steam Society Museum 21/2 miles east of SR 39 on CR 1000 North, Michigan City, Indiana 46360. Stroll by steam-powered trains and cranes, tractors and buzz saws, all still operating today Open Memorial Day weekend Oct. weekends 1-6PM.

Hobart Historical Society Museum 706 E. 4th St., Hobart,Indiana 46342 (Lake). Preserves the colorful history of 19th and 20th Century regional life. Intriguing artifacts from Ice Age fossils and Indian relics to pioneer days. Visit the old blacksmith shop and woodworking shop in this stately historical landmark designed in English Renaissance style. Open Sat. 10AM-3PM, other times by appointment.

Grand Trunk Depot Museum 201 S. Broad, Griffith Indiana 46319 (Lake) Visit an old renovated railroad station full of train memorabilia. Open Jun-Aug Sun. 2-4PM.

Merrillville Historical Museum Open Sundays, 1-4PM during the summer and autumn months. The museum is located in the old Merrillville Town Hall, formerly a school building, 13 W. 73rd Ave. For more information call 769-8312, 755-0078 or 769-8027.

Old Lighthouse Museum Washington Park, Heisman Harbor Road, Michigan City Indiana 46360 (LaPorte). See lighthouse artifacts, Lakefront lore, and a rare 4th Order Fresnel lens. Open daily except Mon. and holidays, 1-4PM.

Porter County Historical Museum 153 S. Franklin St., Valparaiso Indiana 46383 (Porter). Housed in the Old Jail Building, this museum contains interesting artifacts and relics from the area including a WWII monument. Open all year, Tues., Wed., & Fri. 1-4PM.

About the Author:

Robert Flood and his wife, Lorelei, moved from Olympia Fields, Illinois, to Hobart, Indiana, in 2003 upon their retirements. The author is a native Californian whose ancestors on both sides ventured West in the early days by ship, covered wagon and transcontinental railroad.

He grew up on a 52,000-acre grain and cattle ranch in central California's remote back country and directly atop the San Andreas Fault. There he attended a still operational one-room school. In 1958 he graduated in agricultural journalism from California State Polytechnic University, San Luis Obispo, where he edited its campus newspaper.

In 1960 the author relocated to Chicago, where he met his wife, Lorelei, a native Hoosier and Hobart Brickie (class of '54). Until the move to Hobart the author spent more than 40 years as a magazine editor, administrator, freelance writer and marketer.

In 2014 the author formed Country Barn Publishing to specialize in regional history and self-publish **Where the Old West Still Hangs Around,** *celebrating the western heritage of California's San Luis Obispo County. The book has sold more than a thousand copies. More recently he has shifted to the local scene with* **Yesterday is Just Around the Corner.** *The author is a member of the Hobart Kiwanis. He and his wife both volunteer at the Hobart Historical Society.*

Made in the USA
Charleston, SC
01 December 2015